Bloom's

GUIDES

Aldous Huxley's
Brave New World
New Edition

Adventures of Huckleberry Finn
All the Pretty Horses
Animal Farm
The Autobiography of Malcolm X
The Awakening
The Bell Jar
Beloved
Beowulf
Black Boy
The Bluest Eye
Brave New World
The Canterbury Tales
Catch-22
The Catcher in the Rye
The Chosen
The Crucible
Cry, the Beloved Country
Death of a Salesman
Fahrenheit 451
A Farewell to Arms
Frankenstein
The Glass Menagerie
The Grapes of Wrath
Great Expectations
The Great Gatsby
Hamlet
The Handmaid's Tale
Heart of Darkness
The House on Mango Street
I Know Why the Caged Bird Sings
The Iliad
Invisible Man
Jane Eyre

The Joy Luck Club
The Kite Runner
Lord of the Flies
Macbeth
Maggie: A Girl of the Streets
The Member of the Wedding
The Metamorphosis
Native Son
Night
1984
The Odyssey
Oedipus Rex
Of Mice and Men
One Hundred Years of Solitude
Pride and Prejudice
Ragtime
A Raisin in the Sun
The Red Badge of Courage
Romeo and Juliet
The Scarlet Letter
A Separate Peace
Slaughterhouse-Five
Snow Falling on Cedars
The Stranger
A Streetcar Named Desire
The Sun Also Rises
A Tale of Two Cities
Their Eyes Were Watching God
The Things They Carried
To Kill a Mockingbird
Uncle Tom's Cabin
The Waste Land
Wuthering Heights

Bloom's

GUIDES

Aldous Huxley's
Brave New World
New Edition

Edited & with an Introduction
by Harold Bloom

BLOOM'S
LITERARY CRITICISM
An imprint of Infobase Publishing

Bloom's Literary Criticism
An imprint of Infobase Publishing
132 West 31st Street
New York NY 10001

Library of Congress Cataloging-in-Publication Data
Aldous Huxley's Brave new world / edited and with an introduction by Harold Bloom. — New ed.
   p. cm. — (Bloom's guides)
   Includes bibliographical references and index.
   ISBN 978-1-60413-878-8 (hardcover)
   1. Huxley, Aldous, 1894–1963. Brave new world. 2. Dystopias in literature. I. Bloom, Harold.
   PR6015.U9B67245 2010
   823'.912—dc22
                2010028994

Bloom's Literary Criticism books are available at special discounts when purchased in bulk quantities for businesses, associations, institutions, or sales promotions. Please call our Special Sales Department in New York at (212) 967–8800 or (800) 322–8755.

You can find Bloom's Literary Criticism on the World Wide Web at http://www.chelseahouse.com

Contributing editor: Portia Williams Weiskel
Cover designed by Takeshi Takahashi
Composition by IBT Global, Troy NY
Cover printed by IBT Global, Troy NY
Book printed and bound by IBT Global, Troy NY
Date printed: December 2010
Printed in the United States of America
10 9 8 7 6 5 4 3 2 1

This book is printed on acid-free paper.

Contents

Introduction

HAROLD BLOOM

In his foreword to a 1946 edition of *Brave New World* (1931), Aldous Huxley expressed a certain regret that he had written the book when he was an amused, skeptical aesthete rather than the transcendental visionary he had since become. Fifteen years had brought about a world in which there were "only nationalistic radicals of the right and nationalistic radicals of the left," and Huxley surveyed a Europe in ruins after the completion of the Second World War. Huxley himself had found refuge in what he always was to call "the Perennial Philosophy," the religion that is "the conscious and intelligent pursuit of man's Final End, the unitive knowledge of the immanent Tao or Logos, the transcendent godhead or Brahman." As he sadly remarked, he had given his protagonist, the Savage, only two alternatives: to go on living in the Brave New World whose god is Ford (Henry), or to retreat to a primitive Indian village, more human in some ways, but just as lunatic in others. The poor Savage whips himself into the spiritual frenzy that culminates with his hanging himself. Despite Huxley's literary remorse, it seems to me just as well that the book does not end with the Savage saving himself through a mystical contemplation that murmurs "That are Thou" to the Ground of all being.

Sixty-five years after Huxley's foreword, *Brave New World* is at once a bit threadbare, considered strictly as a novel, and more relevant than ever in the era of genetic engineering, virtual reality, and the computer hypertext. Cyberpunk science fiction has nothing to match Huxley's outrageous inventions, and his sexual prophecies have been largely fulfilled. A new technology founded almost entirely on information rather than production, at least for the elite, allies Mustapha Mond and Newt Gingrich, whose orphanages doubtless could have been geared to the bringing up of Huxley's "Bokanovsky groups." Even Huxley's intimation that "marriage licenses will be sold like dog licenses, good for a period of twelve months" was being seriously considered in California not so long ago. It is true that Huxley expected (and feared) too much from the "peaceful" uses of atomic energy, but that is one of his few failures in secular prophecy. The god of the Christian Coalition may not exactly be Our Ford, but he certainly is the god whose worship assures the world without end of Big Business.

Rereading *Brave New World* for the first time in several decades, I find myself most beguiled by the Savage's passion for Shakespeare, who provides the novel with much more than its title. Huxley, with his own passion for Shakespeare, would not have conceded that Shakespeare could have provided the Savage with an alternative to a choice between an insane utopia and a barbaric lunacy. Doubtless, no one ever has been saved by reading Shakespeare or by watching him performed, but Shakespeare, more than any other writer, offers a possible wisdom as well as an education in irony and the powers of language. Huxley wanted his Savage to be a victim or scapegoat, quite possibly for reasons that Huxley himself never understood. *Brave New World*, like Huxley's earlier and better novels *Antic Hay* and *Point Counter Point*, is still a vision of T.S. Eliot's *The Waste Land*, of a world without authentic belief and spiritual values. The author of *Heaven and Hell* and the anthologist of *The Perennial Philosophy* is latent in *Brave New World*, whose Savage dies in order to help persuade Huxley himself that he needs a reconciliation with the mystical Ground of all being.

Biographical Sketch

Aldous Leonard Huxley was born on July 6, 1894, in Godalming in Surrey, England. He came from a family of distinguished scientists and writers: His grandfather was Thomas Henry Huxley, the great proponent of evolution, and his brother was Julian Sorrell Huxley, who became a leading biologist. Aldous attended the Hillside School in Godalming and then entered Eton in 1908, but he was forced to leave in 1910 when he developed a serious eye disease that left him temporarily blind. In 1913, he partially regained his sight and entered Balliol College, Oxford.

Around 1915, Huxley became associated with a circle of writers and intellectuals who gathered at Lady Ottoline Morell's home, Garsington Manor House, near Oxford; there he met T.S. Eliot, Bertrand Russell, Osbert Sitwell, and other figures. After working briefly in the War Office, Huxley graduated from Balliol in 1918 and the next year began teaching at Eton. He was, however, not a success there and decided to become a journalist. Moving to London with his wife, Maria Nys, a Belgian refugee whom he had met at Garsington and married in 1919, Huxley wrote articles and reviews for the *Athenaeum* under the pseudonym Autolycus.

Huxley's first two volumes were collections of poetry, but it was his early novels—*Crome Yellow* (1921), *Antic Hay* (1923), and *Those Barren Leaves* (1925)—that brought him to prominence. By 1925, he had also published three volumes of short stories and two volumes of essays. In 1923 Huxley and his wife and son moved to Europe, where they traveled widely in France, Spain, and Italy. A journey around the world in 1925–26 led to the travel book *Jesting Pilate* (1926), just as a later trip to Central America produced *Beyond the Mexique Bay* (1934). *Point Counter Point* (1928) was hailed as a landmark in its incorporation of musical devices into the novel form. Huxley developed a friendship with D. H. Lawrence, and from 1926 until Lawrence's death in 1930, Huxley spent much time looking after him during his illness with tuberculosis; in 1932 he edited Lawrence's letters.

In 1930, Huxley purchased a small house in Sanary, in southern France. It was there that he wrote one of his most celebrated works, *Brave New World* (1932), a negative utopian or "dystopian" tale that depicted a nightmarish vision of the future in which science and technology are used to suppress human freedom.

Huxley became increasingly concerned about the state of civilization as Europe lurched toward war in the later 1930s: He openly espoused pacifism and (in part through the influence of his friend Gerald Heard) grew increasingly interested in mysticism and Eastern philosophy. These tendencies were augmented when he moved to Southern California in 1937. With Heard and Christopher Isherwood, Huxley formed the Vedanta Society of Southern California, and his philosophy was embodied in such volumes as *The Perennial Philosophy* (1945) and *Heaven and Hell* (1956).

During World War II, Huxley worked as a scenarist in Hollywood, writing the screenplays for such notable films as *Pride and Prejudice* (1941) and *Jane Eyre* (1944). This experience led directly to Huxley's second futuristic novel, *Ape and Essence* (1948), a misanthropic portrait of a postholocaust society written in the form of a screenplay.

In California, Huxley associated with Buddhist and Hindu groups, and in the 1950s he experimented with hallucinogenic drugs such as LSD and mescaline, which he wrote about in *The Doors of Perception* (1954). *Brave New World Revisited* (1958), a brief treatise that discusses some of the implications of his earlier novel, extended the author's pessimism about future society, particularly in the matters of overpopulation and the threat of totalitarianism. But in *Island* (1962)—the manuscript that Huxley managed to save when a brush fire destroyed his home and many of his papers in 1961—he presents a positive utopia in which spirituality is developed in conjunction with technology.

Late in life, Huxley received many honors, including an award from the American Academy of Letters in 1959 and election as a Companion of Literature of the British Royal Society of Literature in 1962. His wife died in 1955, and the next year he married Laura Archera, a concert violinist. Aldous Huxley died of cancer of the tongue on November 22, 1963, the same day as John F. Kennedy and C.S. Lewis.

The Story Behind the Story

Aldous Huxley's decision to merge science with literature seems an obvious choice when one considers his heritage. He was born in 1894 in Surrey, England, and his father, Leonard Huxley, was editor of *Cornhill* magazine, a literary journal that published authors such as George Eliot; Thomas Hardy; Alfred, Lord Tennyson; and Robert Browning. His mother, Julia Arnold, was the niece of the poet Matthew Arnold, and her sister, Mary Humphrey Ward, was a popular novelist in her own right. Huxley's grandfather was the famous biologist T. H. Huxley, Charles Darwin's disciple and protégé.

As it was proper for the son of two such distinguished intellectual families, Huxley attended Eton with the hopes of following in the footsteps of his grandfather and elder brother Julian by becoming a doctor and scientist. Such dreams were dashed when Huxley was 16, as he contracted a serious disease that left him completely blind for two years and seriously damaged his vision for the rest of his life. Huxley changed career paths and in 1916 received his undergraduate degree in literature from Balliol College, Oxford.

Huxley began writing professionally in 1920 for various magazines and published his first novel, *Crome Yellow*, in 1920 at the age of 26. His satirical voice was well-received, and he went on to publish several more novels, producing *Point Counter Point* in 1928, establishing himself as a best-selling author. Although it has not been Huxley's most enduring novel, many critics believe *Point Counter Point* to be his most ambitious and successful work. It was on the heels of this success that Huxley produced *Brave New World*.

Brave New World sold 13,000 copies in England in its first year, 3,000 more than *Point Counter Point*. Although the novel was a success in terms of sales, reviews were uniformly negative. Because it was a departure from his previously lively, "carnivalesque" style, critics accused *Brave New World* of being dry, boring, and overly simplistic. His vision of the future was seen as interesting but irrelevant and unoriginal. In his journal

Books, M. C. Dawson called the novel "a lugubrious and heavy-handed piece of propaganda." Illustrating the attitude of many reviewers, the following is an excerpt from the *New Statesman and Nation*:

[T]his squib about the future is a thin little joke, epitomized in the undergraduate jest of a civilization dated A.F., and a people who refer reverently to 'our Ford'—not a bad little joke, and what it lacks in richness Mr. Huxley tries to make up by repetition; but we want rather more to a prophecy than Mr. Huxley gives us. . . . The fact is Mr. Huxley does not really care for the story—the idea alone excites him. There are brilliant, sardonic little splinters of hate aimed at the degradation he has foreseen for our world; there are passages in which he elaborates conjectures and opinions already familiar to readers of his essays. . . . There are no surprises in it; and if he had no surprises to give us, why should Mr. Huxley have bothered to turn this essay in indignation into a novel?

The reviewer finds "prophecy" in Huxley's novel and is disappointed with the simplicity of it. But Huxley insisted that *Brave New World* was not a prophetic novel but a cautionary one. He saw the rapid changes that scientific advancement was allowing in his society and, aided by a strong scientific background, imagined how much further it might go. In a 1962 interview, Huxley defends his purpose in writing the novel:

[Technology could] iron [humans] into a kind of uniformity, if you were able to manipulate their genetic background . . . if you had a government unscrupulous enough you could do these things without any doubt. . . . We are getting more and more into a position where these things *can* be achieved. And it's extremely important to realize this, and to take every possible precaution to see they shall *not* be achieved. This, I take it, was the message of the book—*This is possible: for heaven's sake be careful about it.*

Another complaint was Huxley's "preoccupation with sexuality." The promiscuity of Huxley's futuristic society, and the ease with which he discusses it, was shocking and disturbing. A reviewer from London's *Times Literary Supplement* wrote, "it is not easy to become interested in the scientifically imagined details of life in this mechanical Utopia. Nor is there compensation in the amount of attention that [Huxley] gives to the abundant sex life of these denatured human beings."

Huxley composed *Brave New World* in 1931, when Europe and America were still reeling—economically, politically, and socially—from World War I. Massive industrialization, coupled with severe economic depression and the rise of fascism, were the backdrop for the novel. It was this turbulence that informed Huxley's cautionary vision of the future. But the massive destruction of World War II was yet to be seen, and Huxley's imagined history of the Nine Years' War and the persecution that followed might have seemed a bit fantastical.

A decade later, the strength of totalitarian states such as Nazi Germany and the Soviet Union, coupled with the terror of World War II, radically changed the world's vision of future possibilities. Huxley's warning of an all-powerful government was more relevant than Dawson thought in 1932. In the second half of the twentieth century, advances in biology were so vast that a eugenic society became more than a mad Englishman's far-fetched fantasy. And today, with the development of successful experiments in cloning, Huxley's tale of caution has somehow morphed into one of prophecy. Even Huxley, in his introduction to a 1946 edition of *Brave New World*, admits:

All things considered it looks as though Utopia were far closer to us than anyone, only fifteen years ago, could have imagined. Then, I projected it six hundred years into the future. Today it seems quite possible that the horror may be upon us within a single century. . . . Indeed, unless we choose to decentralize and to use applied science, not as the end to which human beings are to be made the means, but as the means to producing a race of free individuals, we have only two alternatives to choose from: either a number of national, militarized totalitarianisms, having as their root the terror of the atomic bomb and as their consequence the destruction of civilization . . . or else one supranational totalitarianism, called into existence by the social chaos resulting from rapid technological progress in general and the atomic revolution in particular, and developing, under the need for efficiency and stability, into the welfare-tyranny of Utopia. You pays your money and you takes your choice.

Each decade brings its technological advances, and these advances inexorably alter the social fabric of the world. Perhaps Huxley's guesses were simply lucky, but his utopia seems closer every day. This ability of *Brave New World* to become *more* relevant as time passes accounts for its continual popularity, both as a period piece and as an ever-modern novel.

▮▮ List of Characters

The **Director of Hatcheries and Conditioning for Central London** is the head of the Central Hatchery, where many of the characters work and much of the narrative takes place. He introduces the reader to the facility and the fundamentals of Huxley's futuristic society. It is the director's accident while visiting the Savage Reservation years earlier that provides the impetus for the second half of the novel.

Henry Foster is one of Lenina's boyfriends and accompanies the director on the student tour of the Central Hatchery and Conditioning Centre in the first section of the novel. He serves as a counterpoint to Bernard Marx—where Bernard is antisocial, eccentric, and individual, Henry is the model conditioned citizen.

Lenina Crowne works in the Central Hatchery and Conditioning Centre and accompanies Bernard to the Savage Reservation in New Mexico. Her beauty attracts John, and she becomes the object of his romantic and possessive love. She serves as the liaison between civilized and savage society, as she feels a strong connection for John but is confused by what seems to be a growing predilection for monogamy and love. John's attraction to her, and her inability to abandon the promiscuous dictates of her conditioning, serves as a major conflict during John's visit to London.

Mustapha Mond is one of 10 World Controllers, and his sphere of influence includes England. His position as one of the major upholders of conditioned society is complicated by his understanding of the sacrifice necessary for such a strict society; his secret stash of forbidden religious and literary texts, as well as his personal history as a young man faced with exile or the renunciation of his pursuit of knowledge, demonstrate that individual awareness has not been eradicated in the "civilized" world but merely suppressed.

Bernard Marx is an example of unsuccessful, or incomplete, conditioning. Perhaps due to an accident of his conditioning while he was still "bottled," Bernard is physically imperfect, melancholy, and dissatisfied with life in London. Rather than regularly taking soma and engaging in state-supervised entertainment, he complains about London's lack of individuality and feels an outsider in a society that purports to abolish self-consciousness. He is responsible for bringing John and Linda to London and is finally exiled as a result of his predilection for criticism of the state.

Fanny Crowne also works in the Conditioning Centre and is Lenina's friend. She serves as a warning voice when Lenina exhibits a desire for monogamy, first with Henry Foster and later with John. When Lenina considers the strange passion she feels for John, Fanny counsels her to date and sleep with him and explains Lenina's surprising depression as evidence that she needs a Violent Passion Surrogate. Like Henry, Fanny is a model citizen and cannot contemplate behaving against her conditioning.

Helmholtz Watson feels like an outsider in conditioned society. He writes propaganda for several state-sanctioned publications but longs to write something more meaningful and passionate. He immediately befriends John and is enthralled by the forbidden writings of Shakespeare (which John reveals to him). Like Bernard, he is ultimately exiled by Mond to the Falkland Islands, where he can pose no threat to the stability of conditioned society; unlike Bernard, Helmholtz anticipates his exile as an opportunity to escape the limited society of London and looks forward to having the freedom to explore his individuality in writing.

Linda is the Beta Minus who accompanies the Director to the Savage Reservation decades before the novel's time frame. She is lost during a storm and is left in New Mexico, where she is rescued by an Indian tribe. She is pregnant at the time of her accident, and without the availability of London's abortion centres, is forced to viviparously give birth to the son of the Director. She never fully adjusts to uncivilized life and struggles to adapt her conditioned mind to unconditioned society.

John is the son of Linda and the Director, born on the Savage Reservation. He presents a unique problem, as he is the son (in itself, an abomination) of a conditioned woman who tries to condition him as best she can outside of the technology of London, but he is raised in an unconditioned society. The result is John's inability to complete identify or fit into either world. This becomes clear when he accompanies Bernard to London and is viewed as sideshow entertainment, both fascinating and foreign because of his tendency to form passionate and monogamous attachments to his mother and Lenina. Civilized society has no place for the uncivilized, but neither does the Savage Reservation have a place for someone born to a civilized woman. His lack of place, and therefore lack of identity, is one of the major themes of the novel.

Summary and Analysis

The novel opens at the main entrance of the Central London Hatchery and Conditioning Centre, over which is emblazoned the motto of the World State: "COMMUNITY, IDENTITY, STABILITY." This echoes in form, yet contradicts in meaning, the motto of the French Revolution: "LIBERTY, EQUALITY, FRATERNITY." Immediately the reader is aware that this story is to be an ironic one, and the world in which it is set is not of the democratic vision fought for in late eighteenth-century France.

The narrative begins as the Director of the Central Hatchery (never named beyond his title) leads a tour of young students through the facility in **chapter 1**. Huxley cleverly allows the reader an introduction to his futuristic world by allowing us to follow the narrative from the perspective of one of these students. The Director conducts us through the whole facility in order to give the students a general idea of the complete process of Hatching and Conditioning: "For of course some sort of general idea they must have, if they were to do their work intelligently—though as little of one, if they were to be good and happy members of society, as possible. For particulars, as every one knows, make for virtue and happiness; generalities are intellectually necessary evils. Not philosophers but fretsawyers and stamp collectors compose the backbone of society."

Huxley uses this tour as a realistic way to introduce the reader to the futuristic world he has created. The story takes place in A.F. 632, corresponding to A.D. 2540 (A.F. standing for a new system of dating that is explained in chapter 3).

The tour begins in the Fertilizing Room, where the Director outlines the basic method of fertilization. Selected women are paid the equivalent of six months' salary to undergo an operation in which an ovary is excised and kept "alive and actively developing." As such, the ovary will continue to produce eggs (ova) in its laboratory environment. Each egg is carefully inspected for abnormalities, and if it passes scrutiny, it is then placed in a container with several other ova and is immersed in a high concentration of spermatozoa. The eggs remain in the solution until each is fertilized, after which they are all returned to the incubators.

Here Huxley first introduces the idea of the caste system, seemingly based on the Indian system with which Huxley, as a citizen of the British Empire, would be quite familiar. People belong to one of five castes, Alpha being the most respected and Epsilon being the least: Alpha, Beta, Gamma, Delta, or Epsilon (each caste is then divided into three stratums: for example, Alpha Plus, Alpha, and Alpha Minus). Castes are determined before fertilization; Alpha and Beta ova remain in their incubators until they are "bottled" (explained below), but Gamma, Delta, and Epsilon ova are removed from their incubators so that they may undergo Bokanovsky's Process. "One egg, one embryo, one adult—normality. But a bokanovskified egg will bud, will proliferate, will divide. From eight to ninety-six buds, and every bud will grow into a full-sized adult. Making ninety-six human beings grow where only one grew before." The Director explains to the students (and the reader): "Essentially bokanovskification consists of a series of arrests of development. We check the normal growth and, paradoxically enough, the egg responds by budding." Thus one fertilized egg produces up to 96 identical twins.

One student asks the Director what advantage bokanovskification provides. The Director explains that "Bokanovsky's Process is one of the major instruments of social stability!" Ideally, the entire working class would be composed of one enormous Bokanovsky Group, giving an unheard-of stability to one's identity and, by extension, to one's society (recall the planetary motto of "COMMUNITY, IDENTITY, STABILITY"). Originally, mass production of twins was hindered only by the "ninety-six buds per ova" limit but also by the length of time needed by an ovary to produce eggs. At a normal rate of production, an ovary may produce 200 eggs over 30 years, but the goal of mass production is to yield as many identical (or nearly identical) offspring as possible in the shortest amount of time. Podsnap's Technique, allowing one ovary to produce 150 mature eggs in only two years, quickens the process: "you get an average of nearly eleven thousand brothers and sisters in a hundred and fifty batches of identical twins, all within two years of the same age."

The narrator describes Bokanovsky's Process as logical and rational: "The principle of mass production at last applied to biology." While this statement is not overtly judgmental or even ironic, one must remember that Huxley wrote the novel in the early 1930s, just as industrialization was beginning to affect and dominate the average man's life. While it is dangerous to make too many assumptions about an author's undocumented feelings about specific events, it is safe to assume that *any* person living at that time would have been more than a little anxious about the rapidly changing fabric of daily life. It is not difficult to see how an imagination as active as Huxley's was able to take this common anxiety and the rate at which industry was moving toward mass production and imagine the endpoint of such "progress." In many ways, *Brave New World* demonstrates the result of transplanting the growing ideals of mass production onto humanity itself, rather than simply humanity's machines. This is something to keep in mind throughout the novel; the narrator's opinion of the society that he describes becomes more obvious as the story progresses.

The Director introduces Henry Foster to the students and asks him to explain the record number of production for a single ovary. Henry explains that London's record is 16,012 but that in tropical centers they have reached as high as 17,000. However, he is quick to point out that the "negro ovary" responds much faster to the process. The Director invites Henry to join him in leading the students, and they move on to the Bottling Room.

Huxley describes the Bottling Room as a production line in a factory (indeed, his Hatchery and Conditioning Centre is little more than a factory that produces socialized humans). First, he describes the Liners: A device lifts "flaps of fresh sow's peritoneum ready cut to the proper size" from the Organ Store, and the Liners take each flap and place it on the bottom of a bottle. This is the first step in constructing an artificial womb for the fertilized ova. Next, the Matriculators carefully slit the peritoneal lining, insert the ova, and fill the bottle with a saline solution. Finally, the Labelers tag the bottles with the ova's heredity, date of fertilization, and membership of Bokanovsky Group. "No longer anonymous, but named, identified, the procession marched slowly on into the Social Predestination Room."

The Director, Henry, and the students follow the bottles in the Social Predestination Room, which is a sort of library/research center that determines how many of which caste should be produced at which time. The Social Predestinators control the Decanting Rate, effectively controlling the population. Henry jokes, "If you knew the amount of overtime I had to put in after the last Japanese earthquake!" The Predestinators send their information to the Fertilizers, who then give them the number and caste of embryos requested. After the bottles are "predestined in detail," they are sent to the Embryo Store, the next stop on our tour of the facility.

The Embryo Store is warm and very dark, for as Henry explains to the students, "Embryos are like photographic film. . . . They can only stand red light." Huxley describes the store: "And in effect the sultry darkness into which the students now followed him was visible and crimson, like the darkness of closed eyes of a summer afternoon. The bulging flanks of row on receding row and tier above tier of bottles glinted with innumerable rubies, and among the rubies moved the dim red spectres of men and women with purple eyes and all the symptoms of lupus. The hum and rattle of machinery faintly stirred the air." Each bottle was placed on a rack when it arrived from the Social Predestination Room, and each rack was a slow-moving conveyer belt traveling at 33 centimeters per hour. Various chemicals and hormones are injected into the embryo at specific positions on the conveyer; for example, every embryo is installed with "artificial maternal circulation" at Metre 112, and every bottle is shaken into familiarity with movement during the last two meters of every eight. Each bottle travels exactly 2,136 meters before it is decanted, or "born."

This decanting provokes the narrator to make his first overt judgment on the process and society he is describing; embryos are decanted into "Independent existence—so called." Huxley suggests that once an embryo has been created from stock reproductive organs of a certain caste and then predestined for specific climates, likes and dislikes, and occupations, "independent existence" has become impossible. The reader is reminded of the irony of the World State's motto and realizes the depth of the narrator's ironic judgment.

Henry explains the method of sterilization used in the Embryo Store to the students. Thirty percent of female embryos are allowed to develop normally so they will mature with a fertile reproductive system. Henry points out that one fertile ovary per 1,200 would be sufficient to continue current levels of reproduction. However, 30 percent assures the Hatchery an excellent selection of genetic material. There is no risk of a genetically defective ovary being harvested and used to produce 15,000 ova. The remaining 70 percent of female embryos are injected with male sex hormone every 24 meters, starting at Metre 200. These will become sterile females, or freemartins.

The embryos are conditioned in numerous ways while on the conveyer belts: Those destined to become Epsilons and Deltas are given less oxygen, thus stunting their neurological and physical growth. The Director asks the students, "Hasn't it occurred to you that an Epsilon embryo must have an Epsilon environment as well as an Epsilon heredity?" Embryos undergo heat conditioning, preparing them physically to work in specific latitudes: "Later on their minds would be made to endorse the judgment of their bodies."

Huxley's futuristic society is compelling because it is imperfect; it is still in the throes of scientific investigation and is still seeking ways to make the reproductive process more efficient. Henry suggests the advantage of producing humans who are completely mature in a shorter time span and explains Pilkington's experiments in Mombasa. Pilkington was able to manufacture individuals who were sexually mature at four and physically mature at six-and-a-half. However, he had been unable to speed the mental maturation, so the result was a useless one of adults "too stupid to do even Epsilon work." Henry's tone is one of regret and hopefulness; it is obvious that the discovery of a method to speed maturation would be as significant as Bokanovsky and Podsnap's discoveries.

The tour group comes upon a particularly pretty nurse with whom Henry is acquainted; he introduces the students to Lenina Crowne. Upon Henry's request, Lenina explains that she is injecting embryos with typhoid and sleeping sickness inoculations at Metre 150; these embryos are predestined to work in the Tropics, and immunizing them at such an early stage of development ensures that they are safe from such tropical diseases. Henry explains to the students, "We immunize the fish against the future man's disease."

After viewing the conditioning of future chemical workers (so that they may tolerate lead, caustic soda, tar, and chlorine) and future rocket-plane engineers (whose bottles are kept in constant rotation to improve their sense of balance), the students begin to head toward the conditioning of Alpha Plus Intellectuals, the highest stratum of the highest caste. In the interest of time, however, the Director prevents the students and the readers from viewing that conditioning, thus denying us the knowledge of such procedures. One recalls his previous statement that, while one must be given some sort of general idea of the whole, it is dangerous for individuals to focus too much on generalities. Perhaps the students (and, by extension, the reader) have been given as much of an overview of fertilization and embryonic development as is safe for their limited intellectual development.

While chapter 1 focuses on the conditioning and development of individual embryos, **chapter 2** moves on to describe the further socialization of decanted human beings. The student tour (leaving Henry Foster in the Decanting Room) proceeds from the Embryo Store to the Infant Nurseries. The first stop is in the Neo-Pavlovian Conditioning Rooms, where infants are conditioned to associate certain objects with fear, thus guaranteeing their dislike of said objects throughout their adult lives. This method of conditioning draws from the work of Ivan Pavlov, a Russian scientist of the late nineteenth and early twentieth century. Through his study of the behavior of dogs, Pavlov demonstrated the existence of "conditioned reflexes," or responses that seem instinctive to an adult but are actually the result of some previous, repetitive association.

The students follow the Director into a large sunny room in which a handful of nurses are setting out bowls of roses in a long row across the middle of the room. Between each bowl they place "nursery quartos opened invitingly each at some gaily coloured image of beast or fish or bird." Once the roses and books are laid out in a row, the nurses bring in a Bokanovsky Group of eight-month-old Delta babies. The infants are placed on the floor and immediately begin to crawl toward the flowers and books with "little squeals of excitement, gurgles and twitterings of pleasure." Once all the children are happily engaged with the toys, the Head Nurse presses a lever, signaling a shrieking siren and alarm bells. The children are terrified, but the lesson is not complete until it is cemented with electric shock: "[The Director] waved his hand again, and the Head Nurse pressed a second lever. The screaming of the babies suddenly changed its tone. There was something desperate, almost insane, about the sharp spasmodic yelps to which they now gave utterance. Their little bodies twitched and stiffened; their limbs moved jerkily as if to the tug of unseen wires." The Director explains to the students that the Nurse is able to electrify the entire strip of floor. After the alarms and electricity cease, the children are again offered the books and roses, but this time they are terrified by the sight. This exercise will be repeated 200 times while the infants are in the nursery, forever linking terror and pain with books and flowers. The Director assures the students, "They'll be safe from books and botany all their lives."

The students understand the necessity of conditioning the lower castes to despise books (as too much learning is dangerous), but one boy asks the purpose of adding flowers to the drill. The Director explains that, while flowers themselves pose no threat to the individual or the society, they "have one grave defect: they are gratuitous. A love of nature keeps no factories busy." Originally, the lower castes had been conditioned to love flowers and nature so that they would be compelled to travel to the country in their free time. However, it was not long before another, more economically sound method was developed to lure the people into using mass transport into the country. "We condition the masses to hate the country, but simultaneously we condition them to love all country sports. At the same time, we see to it that all country sports entail the use of elaborate apparatus. So that they consume manufactured articles as well as transport."

The Director changes the subject, telling the students the story of Reuben Rabinovitch, a boy who lived hundreds of years ago in old viviparous days. The students are embarrassed by the thought of viviparous reproduction (i.e., reproduction resulting from sexual contacts between parents), and they have only a partial understanding of "sex," "parents," "birth," and "homes." The Director soothes their embarrassment: "These are unpleasant facts; I know it. But then most historical facts *are* unpleasant. . . . For you must remember that in those days of gross viviparous reproduction, children were always brought up by their parents and not in State Conditioning Centres." The story of Reuben is such: One night his parents accidentally left the radio playing in his bedroom while he slept. The next morning, Polish-speaking Reuben (the Director pauses to remind the students that "Polish," like "French" and "German," is a dead language) was able to recite perfectly, in English, George Bernard Shaw's speech on his own genius, which had been playing on the radio while he slept. Reuben's experience led to the discovery of hypnopaedia, or sleep-teaching.

It took nearly 200 years for hypnopaedia to be used officially, because experiments attempted to use it for "intellectual education"; these experiments failed miserably, as children would wake up able to recite passages of scientific information, but they were unable to understand the meaning of the recitation. "Quite rightly. You can't learn a science unless you know what it's all about." Hypnopaedia was useless until it was applied to "moral education," which, the Director proclaims, "ought never, in any circumstances, to be rational."

While explaining hypnopaedia to the students, the Director says, "'The case of Little Reuben occurred only twenty-three years after Our Ford's first T-Model was put on the market.'

Here the Director made a sign of the T on his stomach and all the students reverently followed suit.'" This is the novel's first mention of "Ford," and although it seems incongruous, the close reader will infer that the Director speaks of Henry Ford, the American inventor and businessman who founded Ford Motors. Furthermore, the reader may notice the religious symbolism of the "sign of the T" and recall the date offered in chapter 1: A.F. 632. Huxley's society has substituted Henry Ford for Jesus Christ and the symbol of the T-Model automobile for that of the crucifix, which will be discussed later in this section.

The Director leads the students into another room, a dormitory filled with 80 Beta boys and girls sleeping in cots. The students are instructed to be silent, and they listen to the hypnopaedic lesson ("Elementary Class Consciousness") broadcast from a speaker underneath each child's pillow:

Alpha children wear grey. They work much harder than we do, because they're so frightfully clever. I'm really awfully glad I'm a Beta, because I don't work so hard. And then we are much better than the Gammas and Deltas. Gammas are stupid. They all wear green, and Delta children wear khaki. Oh no, I don't want to play with Delta children. And Epsilons are still worse. They're too stupid to be able to read or write. Besides they wear black, which is such a beastly colour. I'm so glad I'm a Beta.

This lesson will be repeated 120 times per week for 30 months, more than 15,000 times in total. Once this lesson is cemented, the children will move on to a more advanced "Class Consciousness" lesson. Furthermore, this is only one of many different lessons hynopaedically taught to the children as they mature. The Director lectures: "Till at last the child's mind *is* these suggestions, and the sum of the suggestions *is* the child's mind. And not the child's mind only. The adult's mind—all his life long. The mind that judges and desires and decides—made up of these suggestions. But all these suggestions are *our* suggestions!"

Chapter 3 is composed of three different stories, all occurring simultaneously within the Hatchery. Each story follows a character and will be referred to as plots 1, 2, and 3 (numbered according to the order in which each plot is introduced). The chapter jumps between the three stories throughout; by the end of the chapter, it is rare that two consecutive sentences follow the same plot. For this summary, I have mapped each plotline as though it were independent, and here I will track each separately. It is important to remember, however, that the stories are happening at the same time. By constantly demonstrating the temporal location of each story in relation to the other two, Huxley is able to draw connections and contrasts between them.

The tour skips to another location, now on the playground outside of the Hatchery in plot 1. Hundreds of children are playing games such as Centrifugal Bumble-puppy, which of course requires a massive amount of apparatus to play, therefore increasing consumption as well as providing entertainment. Many other children, around seven or eight years old, are involved in erotic exploration and "rudimentary sexual games." While in the previous chapter the students were embarrassed and horrified by the inappropriateness of mothers and fathers, sexual activity that does *not* result in reproduction is acceptable and even encouraged. The students watch a nurse pull a crying young boy out from behind a bush, followed by a concerned young girl. The nurse explains that she is taking the boy to the psychology department because he is reluctant to join in the expected erotic play. The Director comforts the girl, Polly Trotsky, and sends her back to play. The students are astonished when the Director tells them that in Ford's day, erotic play was suppressed among children and young adults.

The group is surprised by the appearance of Mustapha Mond, the Resident Controller for Western Europe, one of only 10 World Controllers. Mond reminds the students of Our Ford's famous saying, "History is bunk," and uses it as support for the World State's refusal to teach anything historical. While Mond speaks of history, the Director worries that he is treading dangerously close to verbalizing blasphemy: "The D.H.C. looked at him nervously. There were those strange rumours of old forbidden books hidden in a safe in the Controller's study.

Bibles, poetry—Ford knew what." Intuiting the Director's thoughts, Mond turns to him: "'It's all right Director,' he said in a tone of faint derision, 'I won't corrupt them.'"

Mond shocks the students by forcing them to imagine what it must have been like "to have a viviparous mother." He explains the meaning of the word "home" as "a few small rooms, stiflingly over-inhabited. . . . No air, no space; an understerilized prison; darkness, disease, and smells. . . . (The Controller's evocation was so vivid that one of the boys, more sensitive than the rest, turned pale at the mere description and was on the point of being sick.)" He describes a "mother" as a cat: "The mother brooded over her children (*her* children) . . . brooded over them like a cat over its kittens; but a cat that could talk, a cat that could say, 'My baby, my baby,' over and over again."

The Controller then speaks of "our Freud, as for some inscrutable reason, [Ford] chose to call himself whenever he spoke of psychological matters—Our Freud had been the first to reveal the appalling dangers of family life." It appears that in the zealous repudiation of history, even the identity of Henry Ford, their savior, has been confused with a nineteenth-century psychologist.

" . . . Husbands, wives, lovers. There were also monogamy and romance." The students are unfamiliar with any of these terms and are confused because they have been hypnopaedically instructed that "every one belongs to everyone else." (Chapter 3, and the remainder of the novel, is peppered with hypnopaedic proverbs, sometimes identified but often simply a part of a character's vocabulary. These sayings are always short and often have the sound of children's nursery rhymes. Above all, they are instructive in meaning, neat in form, and easy to remember.) This lack of ownership, Mond explains, allows an infinite number of outlets for emotions, effectively reducing the magnitude of any one feeling. He uses the image of pressurized water in a pipe and the magnitude of the jet of water if the pipe is pierced once versus the "piddling little fountains" if it is pierced 20 times. The problem with the "pre-moderns" (Huxley's own society, and our modern world) was its lack of stability: "Mother, monogamy, romance. High spurts in the fountain; fierce and foamy the wild jet. The urge has but a single outlet. . . . No wonder these pre-moderns were mad and wicked and miserable. . . . What with mothers and lovers, what with the prohibitions they were not conditioned to obey . . . they were forced to feel strongly. And feeling strongly (and strongly, what was more, in solitude, in hopelessly individual isolation), how could they be stable?" And stability is "the primal and ultimate need" of society, the reason for development of the Conditioning Centre.

Essentially, Mond argues that all fierce emotion (painful and pleasurable) chips away at individual (and by extension, societal) stability. These uncontrollable urges are the result of "impulse arrested," which must ultimately spill over, "and the flood is feeling, the flood is passion, the flood is even madness." In order to maintain stability, an individual must have no time to notice unfulfilled desire; by shortening the interval between desire and consummation, the World State is able to maintain a stability that would have been impossible in the old days, which not only permitted passion but glorified it.

Mond lectures the students (and conveniently, the reader as well) in the birth of the World State, a birth that was not at all peaceful. Originally, the "reformers" were ignored. "Liberalism," "Parliament," and "democracy" (all words with which the students are unfamiliar) banned ectogenesis (literally, "outside birth"), hypnopaedia, and the Caste System. Mond speaks of the Nine Years' War occurring in A.F. 141 (A.D. 2049), which blasted the planet with chemical warfare, anthrax bombs, poisoned water supplies, and thousands of airplane bombers. Following this armageddon was the great Economic Collapse, leading to a final choice between total destruction or World Control, between stability or chaos.

Huxley's descriptions of this future war are clearly informed by the recent (to him) conclusion of World War I. Shocking the world by its violence and destruction, the war was followed by severe economic problems that showed no signs of easing in 1932, when *Brave New World* was published. Huxley's imagined society holds great relevance for his generation, for it is the result of a social and economic situation that surrounded them already.

It took time, however, for the new government to take hold. The original Controllers attempted to change the social fabric by force, beginning with the conscription of consumption. However, this resulted in a "Back to Nature" movement driven by people who refused to purchase and consume the government-mandated amount of goods per year. Mond points out that this "Back to Nature" movement was also "Back to culture. Yes, actually to culture. You can't consume much if you sit still and read books." The initial government response to these "Simple Lifers" was one of force: In the Golders Green Massacre, 800 objectors were killed by machine guns, and in the British Museum Massacre, 2,000 were "gassed with dichlorethyl sulphide" (mustard gas, which both Huxley and his original audience had learned to fear during the previous decade's World War I).

Ultimately, the Controllers were forced to turn to less violent means: "The slower but infinitely surer methods of ectogenesis, neo-Pavlovian conditioning and hypnopaedia . . . an intensive propaganda campaign against viviparous reproduction . . . accompanied by a campaign against the Past; by the closing of museums, the blowing up of historical monuments (luckily most of them had already been destroyed during the Nine Years' War); by the suppression of all books published before A. F. 150 (A. D. 2058)." And the operation was successful; the Controllers were able to condition the population to accept a new world order. The date of Henry Ford's introduction of the T-Model automobile (1908) was chosen as the "opening date of the new era," and "all crosses had their tops cut off and became T's." Instead of "God," the new society celebrates Ford's Day and sponsors Community Sings and Solidarity Services. And in place of "heaven," "the soul," and "immortality," the World State provides soma, a drug that began to be produced commercially in A.F. 178 (A.D. 2086) and provided "all the advantages of Christianity and alcohol; none of their defects." Soma is used every day by the population and is provided by the State; it gives individuals a "holiday from reality," and its constant supply ensures stability.

The last hurdle the new State had to overcome was the victory over old age. By developing medical technology that prevented physical and mental maturation beyond a certain point, the State is able to guarantee that "characters remain constant throughout a whole lifetime. . . . Work, play—at sixty our powers and tastes are what they were at seventeen. Old men in the bad old days used to renounce, retire, take to religion, spend their time reading, thinking—*thinking!*" Now, however, if an individual does find himself with a spare moment, it is always filled with soma.

As Mond finishes his lecture on old age, two children approach him (the tour is still on the playground). The Director shouts angrily at the children, "Go away, little girl! Go away, little boy! Can't you see that his fordship's busy? Go and do your erotic play somewhere else." "His Fordship" Mustapha Mond responds by whispering to himself, "Suffer little children," alluding to the passage from the Gospel of Mark: "And they brought young children to him, that he should touch them: and his disciples rebuked those that brought them. But when Jesus saw it, he was much displeased, and said unto them, Suffer the little children to come unto me, and forbid them not: for of such is the kingdom of God." With this suggestive yet distorted biblical allusion, the chapter, and the tour, concludes. The reader's last impression of Mond recalls the Director's earlier fears that he keeps a secret stash of forbidden books in his office and hints that perhaps there are cracks in the World State's seemingly flawless map of social stability.

The second story line (plot 2) begins just after Mustapha Mond joins the student tour. It is four o'clock in the afternoon, time for a shift change at the Conditioning Centre. Henry Foster is in the elevator going up to the Men's Changing Rooms. Henry chats with the Assistant Director of Predestination, both of them pointedly ignoring the third man in the elevator due to his "unsavoury reputation." Henry and the Assistant Director talk about the latest show at the Feelies, Huxley's futuristic version of the cinema, a show that includes tactile and olfactory, as well as visual, stimulation. The Assistant Director asks Henry about Lenina, and Henry answers that "she's a splendid girl. Wonderfully pneumatic. I'm surprised you haven't had her." Henry, who has apparently been "having" Lenina for quite some time, suggests that the Assistant Director "have" her at the first opportunity, repeating what is obviously a hypnopaedic lesson: "Every one belongs to every one else, after all." The men continue their gossip, admiring Lenina's friend Fanny Crowne as very attractive but "not nearly so pneumatic as Lenina." "Pneumatic" seems to be the stock word for female attractiveness, yet another example of how imagery of automation, industry, and, of course, anything to do with Henry Ford permeates this futuristic culture.

During this discussion, the ignored third man in the elevator, Bernard Marx, listens. He is contemptuous of them as they discuss the Feelies but turns pale when Henry mentions Lenina. In a departure from what Huxley has conditioned the reader to expect from the inhabitants of his world, Bernard is offended on behalf of Lenina: "Talking about her as though she were a bit of meat. . . . Have her here, have her there. Like mutton. Degrading her to so much mutton." Bernard's sentiments run in opposition to the hypnopaedic lesson recited by Henry; for some reason, he does not seem to instinctively believe that "Every one belongs to every one else." What bothers Bernard most is that Lenina "thinks of herself as meat." In other words, Bernard is upset that Lenina is so normal; for whatever reason, he clearly is not.

Bernard's individuality, coupled with the suggestion of Mond's eccentricities, begins to illuminate a major query of the novel. In this society, which is based wholly upon conformity, what happens to those who are unique? How do they behave toward society? And of course, how does their society deal with them? These questions are more clearly explored later in the novel.

Henry comments on how glum Marx looks and offers him a gram of soma. Bernard refuses (thinking how he despises Henry), but Henry insists, backed by the Assistant Director who mockingly recites yet another hypnopaedic lesson: "One cubic centimetre cures ten gloomy sentiments." They persist until Bernard yells at them, cursing, in response to which the two men laugh and exit the elevator. We see Bernard muttering to himself, "Idiots, swine!" subtly echoing Matthew 7:6, "Give not that which is holy unto the dogs, neither cast ye your pearls before swine, lest they trample them under their feet, and turn again and rend you." The implication is that Bernard is in possession of something far more valuable than Foster or the Assistant Director understand. This individuality is something that Bernard must keep secret from those who are "normal," or else that uniqueness will be "trampled" and then the bearer of it, Bernard himself, will be "rent." The allusion is strengthened by its textual proximity to Mustapha Mond's more direct reference to the Bible. This occurs near the end of the chapter, by which point the different plots are textually layered so that the reader, by alternating between them, is essentially reading them simultaneously (which is, of course, how they are happening). Therefore, both Mustapha's and Bernard's surprising (though not necessarily intentional) biblical references occur at the same time, in different locations, and in different plots.

The third plot revolves around Lenina, beginning again at the shift change. Like Henry, she takes the elevator up to the Girls' Dressing-Room, where she showers and chats with her friend and co-worker Fanny Crowne (the same Fanny discussed by Henry and the Assistant Director). Although they are not members of a Bokanovsky Group, both girls have the same last name, which is not uncommon as "the two thousand million inhabitants of the planet had only ten thousand names between them." Lenina's shower ritual introduces the reader to several futuristic machines, such as the vibro-vacuum massage machine and the synthetic music machine. These inventions are never fully explained, but they seem to be enhanced versions of what would have been very basic devices during Huxley's lifetime: For example, the synthetic music machine is simply a much-improved radio.

Lenina and Fanny discuss their plans for the evening. To Lenina's surprise, Fanny is not going on a date. She explains (it seems that an evening without a date needs explanation) that she's been feeling unwell and that Dr. Wells prescribed a Pregnancy Substitute. While this is not explained in detail, it seems to be a program of injections of ovarin and placentin, intended to provide a hormonal substitute for pregnancy.

Fanny is appalled that Lenina is planning to go out with Henry Foster that night, noting that Lenina and Henry have been going out regularly for four months. Scandalized that Lenina has not gone out with anyone else during this time, Fanny urges her to see other men as well: "Of course there's no need to give him up. Have somebody else from time to time, that's all. He has other girls, doesn't he? . . . Of course he does. Trust Henry Foster to be the perfect gentleman—always correct." Lenina reluctantly agrees but explains that she "hadn't been feeling very keen on promiscuity lately." Fanny is sympathetic but reminds her that she must make the effort, as "every one belongs to every one else."

Lenina confides that Bernard Marx invited her to accompany him on a vacation to the Savage Reservation in New Mexico. Fanny is horrified, citing his reputation for spending time alone ("They say he doesn't like Obstacle Golf.") and his less-than-average physical appearance. She gossips: "They say somebody made a mistake when he was still in the bottle—thought he was a Gamma and put alcohol into his blood-surrogate. That's why he's so stunted." Lenina argues that she finds him "rather sweet. . . . One feels one would like to pet him. You know. Like a cat." This recalls Mond's description of a "mother" as a cat brooding over her kittens; metaphorically, then, Bernard is subtly identified with viviparous existence, rife with passion and exiled from this new society.

Fanny and Lenina's conversation ends with a more light-hearted banter about Lenina's new Malthusian Belt, a gift from Henry Foster. This belt seems to be a stylish vehicle for contraceptives, essential for all females who are not freemartins. Huxley names the belt after Thomas Malthus, a late-eighteenth-, early-nineteenth-century philosopher who observed that nature produces more offspring than can realistically survive. Malthus applied this observation to the human population and argued the necessity for population control as a means to avoid famine and poverty. His ideas were fundamental to Darwin's theory of natural selection.

These are the three main plotlines of chapter 3. As the chapter progresses, the "scenes" get shorter, so that in the last third of the chapter, the scene changes nearly every sentence. At this point, two more scenes are introduced and are interspersed between the three major plotlines. The first is the hypnopaedic lesson, "Adapting future demand to future industrial supply." I've pieced it together as follows: *I do love flying. I do love flying, I do love having new clothes. But old clothes are beastly. We always throw away old clothes. Ending is better than mending, ending is better than mending, ending is better than mending. The more stitches, the less riches; the more stitches, the less riches.*

The fifth scene appears only once, closing the chapter in the Embryo Store: "Slowly, majestically, with a faint humming of machinery, the Conveyors moved forward, thirty-three centimetres an hour. In the red darkness glinted innumerable rubies."

In part 1 of **chapter 4**, Lenina enters the elevator to leave the building and recognizes most of the men coming from the Alpha Changing Room. "She was a popular girl and, at one time or another, had spent a night with almost all of them." She spots Bernard huddled in the corner and loudly accepts his invitation to New Mexico. She notices many of her former dates looking shocked that she would associate with someone as disreputable as Marx, but this disapproval spurs her to speak louder ("she was publicly proving her unfaithfulness to Henry. Fanny ought to be pleased, even though it was Bernard."). Bernard is embarrassed by the attention and blushingly suggests they discuss it elsewhere, when there are fewer people around. Lenina laughs at his eccentricity and the lift arrives at the roof, where its passengers disembark. The sky is humming with helicopters and rocket-planes; air travel seems to be the way of the future. Bernard comments, with a trembling voice, on how beautiful the sky is; Lenina "smiled at him with an expression of the most sympathetic understanding. 'Simply perfect for Obstacle Golf.'" This exchange distills the difference between Bernard and Lenina or, more accurately, the distance between Bernard and the rest of conditioned society. People are not meant to adore beauty for the sake of beauty; beauty exists to channel everything toward consumerism, like it does with Lenina. Lenina waves goodbye to Bernard and runs across the roof toward Henry's helicopter, anxious that he will be angry if she keeps him waiting.

Benito Hoover, a former date of Lenina's, emerges from the elevator behind Bernard and comments on how glum he looks. Like Henry in the previous chapter, Benito offers Bernard a gram of soma, prompting Bernard to rush away.

Lenina reaches Henry's helicopter, where he chastises her for being four minutes late. They lift off and the reader is given an aerial tour of London. We see (with Lenina) the many stadiums and arenas for sports such as Riemann-surface tennis and Escalator Fives. Part 1 ends as Henry and Lenina land at Stoke Poges and begin to play Obstacle Golf.

Part 2 follows Bernard after Lenina leaves him on the roof. He is very upset: angry at Benito for being so good-natured and at Lenina for being so "normal." He was "wretched that she should have thought it such a perfect afternoon for Obstacle Golf, that she should trotted away to join Henry Foster, that she should have found him funny for not wanting to talk of their most private affairs in public. Wretched, in a word, because she had behaved as any healthy and virtuous English girl ought to behave and not in some other, abnormal, extraordinary way." Bernard is aware that he is not quite "normal"; he is physically well below average (his "physique was hardly better than that of the average Gamma"), and this physical inferiority "made him feel an outsider; and feeling an outsider he behaved like one, which increased the prejudice against him and intensified the contempt and hostility aroused by his physical defects." He envies men like Henry and Benito who never feel self-conscious about their appearance, men "so utterly at home as to be unaware either of themselves or of the beneficent and comfortable element in which they had their being."

He boards his helicopter and flies to the Bureaux of Propaganda, where he picks up his friend Helmholtz Watson. Helmholtz works as a lecturer at the College of Emotional Engineering and as a writer for *The Hourly Radio* (an upper-caste newspaper); he also composes Feely scripts and hypnopaedic rhymes. Unlike Bernard, Helmholtz is physically perfect. However, he feels smarter than everyone else, making him an outsider like Bernard: "What the two men shared was the knowledge that they were individuals."

Helmholtz accompanies Bernard to his apartment, where he speaks of a strange urge that he has been unable to identify. The reader easily recognizes this urge as the desire to exert his individuality; Helmholtz is unable to name it, for no matter how intelligent, he is still a conditioned member of society. He asks Bernard, "Did you ever feel as though you had something inside you that was only waiting for you to give it a chance to come out? Some sort of extra power that you aren't using— you know, like all the water that goes down the falls instead of through the turbines?" The image of controlled water echoes Mond's description of emotion in chapter 3 as water spurting roughly from a single puncture in a pipe.

Bernard interrupts Helmholtz, thinking he hears someone at the door. This sort of conversation is forbidden, and so the nervous Bernard checks to make sure they are truly alone. They are, and Bernard is embarrassed at his nerves. He complains to Helmholtz, excusing his behavior by bewailing how suspicious people are of him and how much that makes him suspicious of everyone else. Helmholtz listens but feels a bit ashamed for his friend. "He wished Bernard would show a little more pride."

Huxley takes us back to Stoke Poges in part 1 of **chapter 5**, where it is eight o'clock in the evening. Lenina and Henry board his helicopter and fly back to London, passing over the monorail trains that provide transportation for the lower castes (who presumably cannot afford their own helicopters). They pass the Slough Crematorium, where smokestacks release the chemicals of each human body as it is burned. Not only does the crematorium produce jobs and necessitate industry (as opposed to the materials and labor required by a graveyard), but it also incorporates a phosphorous recovery program, in which 98 percent of the phosphorous emitted from a burning human body is recovered, totaling 400 tons of phosphorous from England each year. Henry perfectly sums up his society's attitude: "Fine to think we can go on being socially useful even after we're dead. Making plants grow."

Lenina has a slightly more creative reaction; she adds: "But queer that Alphas and Betas won't make any more plants grow than those nasty little Gammas and Deltas and Epsilons . . ." Henry answers with a stock response, sounding suspiciously like a hypnopaedic lesson: "All men are physico-chemically equal. . . . Besides, even Epsilons perform indispensable services." One should not ignore the similarity of Henry's statement to the post-Enlightenment sentiment, "All men are created equal." For this, of course, is no longer true in Huxley's world. As they leave the Crematorium behind, neither Henry nor Lenina is disturbed by the thought of death; as Henry repeats, "there's one thing we can be certain of; whoever he may have been, he was happy when he was alive. Everybody's happy now."

Back at Henry's apartment, the couple eats dinner and takes soma with coffee after the meal. They go to the Westminster Abbey Cabaret (Huxley's cathedral ironically transformed into a cabaret) to see the latest Synthetic Music show. All doped up on soma, hundreds of couples dance suggestively to the music; Huxley's language associates the dancing with sexual intercourse and the music with arousal culminating in orgasm. The "musicians," Calvin Stopes and His Sixteen Sexophonists, conclude the show with a song beginning, "Bottle of mine." Unlike twentieth-century songs beginning with similar lyrics, however, the bottle to which they refer is filled not with beer or whiskey but peritoneum lining, blood-surrogate, and carefully engineered embryos.

Henry and Lenina, due to the combination of soma and music, are swept away in the entertainment (they are on a soma-holiday). "Bottled" (drunk), they return to Henry's apartment. As they climb into bed, Lenina, as though by instinct (or conditioning) remembers to take her contraceptives to avoid a viviparous situation.

After dining with Helmholtz, Bernard flies to the Fordson Community Singery for his biweekly Solidarity Service in part

2. He arrives just as Big Henry (as opposed to Big Ben) strikes nine o'clock: He is late. He arrives at Room 3210 (countdown?) just in time, pleased that he is not the last to arrive. Bernard sits next to Morgana Rothschild, and is embarrassed when he must admit to her that he did not spend the afternoon playing Obstacle or Electromagnetic Golf. As the service begins, Bernard is pessimistic about its outcome; he "foresaw for himself yet another failure to achieve atonement." The Solidarity Service, then, seems to be Huxley's answer to going to church. The Service progresses as follows:

The 12 members of the group (reminiscent of the 12 apostles) sit in a circle, alternating males and females. The President of the Group stands, makes the sign of the "T," and switches on the synthetic music. A cup of strawberry ice-cream soma is passed between the 12, each drinking after reciting, "I drink to my annihilation." Three Solidarity Hymns are sung, interspersed with other liturgical recitations: "I drink to the Greater Being," and "I drink to the imminence of His Coming." Each hymn focuses on the coming of the "Greater Being" and the simultaneous merging of individual existence into this Greater Being. Unlike Christian regenerative theology, which begs salvation of the individual through God, Huxley's "religion" seems to call for the annihilation of the individual and the subsequent *creation* of a God, the Greater Being or Twelve-in-One. The supreme deity in Bernard's society is not a larger-than-life individual but the aggregate of all human individuals in one mass being.

After the singing of the hymns, the Solidarity Group engages in a sort of pentecostal frenzy, the synthetic voice instructing them to listen for the feet of the Greater Being. Soon, one of the members (Morgana) jumps up, claiming to hear him, prompting the others to follow suit. Bernard, "feeling that it was time for him to do something . . . also jumped up and shouted, 'I hear him; He's coming.' But it wasn't true. He heard nothing and, for him, nobody was coming." As usual, Bernard is different from his peers; what makes him different is his awareness of his own individuality. He is unable to annihilate himself for the coming of the Twelve-in-One.

The Group dances in circles, becoming more frenetic and now singing "Orgy-porgy," the lyrics of which recall sexual imagery, much as did the music at the Westminster Abbey Cabaret. The lights dim until "they were dancing in the crimson twilight of the Embryo Store," and the service culminates in what appears to be an orgy.

After the service, Fifi Bradlaugh, another member of Bernard's Solidarity Group, approaches him and comments on how wonderful the service was. He agrees with her, but he is lying; he feels "separate and unatoned, while the others were being fused into the Greater Being. . . . [T]he sight of [Fifi's] transfigured face was at once an accusation and an ironical reminder of his own separateness. He was as miserably isolated now as he had been when the service began—more isolated by reason of his unreplenished emptiness, his dead satiety."

In **chapter 6**, part 1, several weeks have passed, and Lenina questions her decision to accompany Bernard to New Mexico. She has gone on several dates with him and finds him increasingly strange. Her other option, however, is returning to the North Pole with George Edzel, which she found quite boring the previous summer. She is ultimately enticed by the opportunity to visit a Savage Reservation, which requires a special permit (Bernard has one) and is quite a rare occurrence (only six people in the entire Conditioning Centre had ever visited one). She confides her worries about Bernard to Fanny, who again claims that his oddness is due to alcohol in his blood-surrogate. Henry, however, refers to Bernard as a "rhinoceros," explaining that some men simply "don't respond properly to conditioning."

Lenina remembers her first date with Bernard: Nixing her suggestion of Electro-Magnetic Golf, Bernard proposes that they go for a long walk, where they can be alone and talk. Lenina is shocked by the suggestion and finally persuades him to fly to Amsterdam and attend the Semi-Demi Finals of the Women's Heavyweight Wrestling Competition. Bernard, of course, has a miserable time. He becomes more and more frustrated with Lenina, who responds to his unhappiness with a number of hypnopaedic rhymes. She tempts him with soma in order to cure his bad mood with the lure, "A gramme is always better than a damn." But Bernard still refuses, arguing, "I'd rather be myself. . . . Myself and nasty. Not somebody else, however jolly."

On this flight back to London, Bernard cuts the engines and hovers the helicopter low above the storming waters of the English Channel, ordering Lenina to look down. She is terrified of the darkness and the silence and urges Bernard to continue flying. He tries to make her understand why he loves looking into the dark water: "It makes me feel as though . . . as though I were more *me*, if you see what I mean. More on my own, not so completely a part of something else. Not just a cell in the social body." Lenina becomes more and more upset, refusing to listen to Bernard as he goes on to talk of his desire to be "free" from his conditioning. Finally, Bernard submits to Lenina's tears, obviously disappointed in her inability to try to understand his thoughts. They return to his rooms, where Bernard takes a large dose of soma, and they go to bed.

The next afternoon, Lenina asks Bernard if he enjoyed himself the night before and is unsettled and confused when he tells her that he wishes they had not slept together on their first date. Again, she cannot understand his reasons and assumes that he means that she was not attractive enough. He explains that he would have liked to try "the effect of arresting [his] impulses," but once more Lenina responds with a hypnopaedic lesson: "Never put off till to-morrow the fun you can have today."

The chapter concludes with Lenina confiding her anxieties to Fanny but still insisting: "All the same . . . I do like him. He has such awfully nice hands. And the way he moves his shoulders—that's very attractive. . . . But I wish he weren't so odd."

In final preparations for his trip to the Savage Reservation, Bernard visits the Director's office to get his signature on the permit in part 2. The Director surprises Bernard by recounting his own visit, years ago, to the New Mexican reservation. Like Bernard, he took a girl there on vacation, but during the night she wandered off and was lost in a huge thunderstorm. The Director himself lost the horses and had to crawl back to the rest house. Although a massive search was conducted, the girl (a Beta Minus) could not be found, and it was concluded that she came upon some mishap in the desert and was killed. The Director tells Bernard how frightening the whole ordeal was and how long he was plagued by nightmares of thunderstorms and the wilderness.

As abruptly as the Director began his tale, he concludes it, embarrassed and angry that he revealed such a "discreditable secret." To cover for his lapse in judgment (and, as he sees it, a revelation of weakness), the Director berates Bernard for his less-than-normal extracurricular activities (that is, his *lack* of activities). He explains that it is Bernard's duty to conform: "Alphas are conditioned that they do not *have* to be infantile in their emotional behaviour. But that is all the more reason for their making a special effort to conform. It is their duty to be infantile, even against their inclination." He completes his lecture by warning Bernard that unless he makes a better effort to conform to societal standards, he will face exile to a Sub-Centre, possibly the one in Iceland.

Bernard leaves the office exalted, feeling as though he emerged from an adventure as the hero. Of course, he is certain that the Director's threats will never actually occur; as such, he is able to revel in his "rebellion" without actually facing any consequences. That evening, Bernard exaggerates the encounter to Helmholtz, who sees his friend's hypocrisy and boasting. As in the previous chapter, Helmholtz is ashamed for Bernard and wishes he were less boastful and self-pitying.

A week later, Bernard and Lenina take the Blue Pacific Rocket to Santa Fe in part 3. They spend the night there and meet with the Warden of the Reservation the following morning. He lectures them on the specifics of the reservation: It covers 560,000 square kilometers and is divided into four Sub-Reservations, each contained by an electric fence that prevents escape (it kills on contact). The reservation contains approximately 60,000 Indians (although it is impossible to keep an accurate count) and preserves viviparous life: marriage, families, religion, extinct languages, infectious disease, ferocious animals, priests. After outlining the makeup of the reservation, the Warden signs their permit and arranges for a Reservation Guard to fly them into the reservation.

While they wait, Bernard telephones Helmholtz because he fears he left a cologne tap running in his apartment. Helmholtz informs him that the Director announced that he was looking for a replacement for Bernard in the Conditioning Centre, hinting that Bernard would be exiled to Iceland. Bernard is terribly upset (not at all like the isolated hero of the previous week when Iceland was just a distant threat) and is anxious to conform if the Director would only give him another opportunity: "He raged against himself—what a fool!—against the Director—how unfair not to give him another chance, that other chance which, he now had no doubt at all, he had always intended to take." This summarizes that hypocrisy that Helmholtz sees in Bernard; as soon as he is actually faced with being an individual, he wishes nothing other than a chance to act as conditioned as Lenina.

Lenina persuades Bernard to take soma, and they board the plane that flies them over the Reservation. Bernard sleeps and wakes only when they land in Malpais, their destination for the afternoon and where they will spend the night. The chapter ends as the helicopter lifts off, leaving them with an Indian guide, but not before the pilot reminds them: "They're perfectly tame; savages won't do you any harm. They've got enough experience of gas bombs to know that they mustn't play any tricks."

In **chapter 7**, Bernard and Lenina climb the mesa to Malpais, following an Indian guide who, Lenina distastefully notices, stinks. Huxley notes that the pueblo looks like a collection of "amputated pyramids," recalling Mond's lecture to the students in which he describes "some things called the pyramids" that were destroyed in the "campaign against the past." Lenina likens this alien world to London: The mesa is "like the Charing-T Tower," and the naked Indians, painted with white lines, remind her of "asphalt tennis courts." She and Bernard are shocked when they witness old age, a phenomenon that has been eradicated from their society. Lenina sees a mother nursing her child and reaches desperately for her soma, only to discover that she left it at the rest house. Presumably for the first time in her life, Lenina must face unpleasantness without soma. The two are led to a terrace from which they can look down into the village square, where a ritual is about to begin. Lenina is comforted by the steady banging of drums, reminding "her reassuringly of the synthetic noises made at Solidarity Services and Ford's Day celebrations." This comfort is short-lived; the ritual is one of pain and blood, and Lenina becomes more and more distraught at the sight of a young man being whipped until he faints.

As the ritual ends, Lenina sits in shock, covering her face with her hands. Bernard turns as a young Indian enters the room, and he is surprised that this Indian, in addition to being blond-haired and blue-eyed, can speak flawless English. The savage, John, is thrilled to meet "civilized" people; he explains that he is the son of a woman who visited the Reservation years ago. Apparently, his mother had fallen while taking a walk, and the Indians had brought her to the pueblo to care for her. Her escort, a man named Tomakin, "must have flown away, back to the Other Place, away without her—a bad, unkind, unnatural man." Bernard immediately realizes that this young man must be the son of the Director (whose first name is Thomas, surprisingly similar to "Tomakin") and his mother the Beta Minus woman he assumed was dead.

John calls his mother, Linda, into the room. Smelling of alcohol (as Lenina observes, she "simply reeked of that beastly stuff that was put into Delta and Epsilon bottles"), grossly overweight, and incredibly dirty, Linda is hysterical at the sight of "civilized" people. She rushes at Lenina and hugs her, nearly making her sick. Bernard and John take a walk outside the house, leaving Linda to fawn over Lenina's silk-acetate clothing and Malthusian belt. She tells Lenina that she found herself to be pregnant after her fall and rescue by the Indians; apparently the Malthusian contraceptives sometimes fail to work, but in the Reservation there are no abortion centres, so Linda was forced to give birth. She tried as best she could to "condition" John, teaching him what hypnopaedic rhymes she remembered as nursery rhymes, attempting to protect him from the insanity of the savages. Linda laments the lack of soma in the Reservation; once reliant on the drug, she had turned to the nearest thing she can find: mescal. While soma is not physically addictive, mescal is, and Linda has become an alcoholic.

The Indians saw Linda as a prostitute, as she could not understand the savage belief in monogamy. In addition to her white skin and strange ways, this turned her and John into something like outcasts. John, for instance, desperately wanted to participate in the coming-of-age ritual witnessed earlier, but he is excluded because of his "complexion." He claims that he would have been a much stronger participant than the boy they chose (the boy who was beaten until unconscious); he says: "They could have had twice as much blood from me. The multitudinous seas incarnadine. . . . But they wouldn't let me. They disliked me for my complexion. It's always been like that. Always." John's reference to Shakespeare is surprising: He alludes to Macbeth's speech in Act II: "Will all great Neptune's ocean wash this blood / Clean from my hand? No, this my hand will rather / The multitudinous seas incarnadine, / Making the green one red." John, half-conditioned, half-savage, somehow knows *Macbeth* well enough to quote it.

The chapter closes with Linda bewailing her condition, specifically her inability to completely civilize her son. Particularly in regard to sexual relations, John's beliefs are those of the Indians rather than those of his mother. Linda tells Lenina: . . . he tried to kill poor Waihusiwa—or was it Popé?—just because I used to have them sometimes. Because I never *could* make him understand that that was what civilized people ought to do. Being mad's infectious, I believe." With this last potentially prophetic statement, the chapter ends.

While Linda bewails her condition to Lenina, Bernard and John speak outside the building in **chapter 8**. Bernard is curious about John's life and begs him to tell his story "from the beginning. As far back as you can remember." What follows is John's first-person narrative of his history, composed of anecdotes and incidents, sometimes with years in between. These memories will be divided into episodes for easier reference.

Episode 1: John is quite young and remembers Linda singing him her version of lullabies to help him fall asleep. Not knowing any traditional lullabies, she sings whatever rhymes she can recall from the "Other Place": "Streptocock-Gee to Banbury-T" and "Bye Baby Banting, soon you'll need decanting." John falls asleep but is awakened by laughing. He sees an Indian man with hair "like two black ropes" in bed with Linda, whispering to her and making her laugh. Frightened, John snuggles against Linda, prompting her to tell the man, "Not with John here." Rather than leaving, however, the man pulls John out of the bed and locks him in a back room. John yells for his mother, but she neither answers nor frees him; she is presumably engaged sexually with the Indian.

Episode 2: Still a child, John plays with Indian boys in the weaving room, while their mothers work the looms. Suddenly, Linda gets into an argument with an Indian woman and is pushed out of the room; John follows her and discovers that she broke something. She says, "How should I know how to do their beastly weaving? Beastly savages." Popé waits for them at their house, and he gives Linda a gourd of mescal, which she quickly drinks and passes out in bed.

Episode 3: John recalls an afternoon he returned to their house to find several Indian women beating Linda. Screaming, he tries to intervene, only to be knocked to the ground and whipped several times himself. That evening, he asks Linda why the women wanted to hurt her. She tells him that she does not really understand but that the women said, "those men are *their* men"; Linda is being punished for her promiscuity, conditioned as "normal" behavior since she was an infant. John tries to hug his mother, but she is repulsed by her "son" and beats him out of frustration, screaming, "Turned into a savage. Having young ones like an animal. . . . If it hadn't been for you, I might have gone to the Inspector, I might have got away. But not with a baby. That would have been too shameful." Linda finally stops hitting John, suddenly hugging and kissing him. This incident, in addition to John's others stories about Linda, illustrates how she is split between her instinct to mother her son and her conditioning to hate all things viviparous. Her conditioning does not seem to have completely wiped out her natural instinct, but it has affected her so that she can never completely love her son.

Episode 4: John's favorite childhood memories are of Linda's stories about the Other Place, or the "civilized" world. He is enchanted by her tales of elaborate games and Feelies, electric lighting and Scent Organs, "and people never lonely, but living together and being so jolly and happy, like the summer dances here in Malpais, but much happier, and the happiness being there every day . . ." Linda's stories are contrasted by the tales of one of the elders in the pueblo, who speaks to the children about the mystical religion of the Indians, which seems to be a fusion of Christianity and nature worship. The two different mythologies combine in John's head: "Lying in bed, he would think of Heaven and London and Our Lady of Acoma and the rows and rows of babies in clean bottles and Jesus flying up and Linda flying up and the great Director of the World hatcheries and Awonawilona."

Episode 5: Linda continues to see many different men, prompting the pueblo to label her a whore. Even the children mocked her, a song of theirs inciting John to throw stones at them. The stone-throwing fight is weighted in favor of the Indian boys and ends with John covered in blood.

Episode 6: Writing simple rhymes on the wall with charcoal, Linda teaches John to read. Once he learns the basics, she gives him the book she had the day she was lost: *The Chemical and Bacteriological Conditioning of the Embryo. Practical Instructions for Beta Embryo-Store Workers*. John is frustrated and bored with the book but begins to see his ability to read as a sort of revenge against the Indian boys who continually mock his mother. Her book raises a number of questions for him, questions that Linda, with her limited and very specific training, is unable to answer. Her explanation for the existence of things is always practical but of no use in the pueblo. For example, she explains that "chemicals" come from bottles that come from the Chemical Store. John is much more intrigued by the Indian explanation for existence: "The seed of men and all creatures, the seed of the sun and the seed of the earth and the seed of the sky—Awonawilona made them all out of the Fog of Increase." Again, John is trained by two opposing worlds, making his viewpoint unique and not entirely acceptable by either society.

Episode 7: Soon after his twelfth birthday, Linda gives John an old book that Popé found in an ancient chest. Linda supposes the book to be "uncivilized" but thinks it must be useful for John to practice his reading. The book is called *The Complete Works of William Shakespeare*. John opens the book at random, and the first passage he reads is from the third act of *Hamlet*, with Hamlet berating his mother for her infidelity: "Nay, but to live / In the rank sweat of an enseamed bed, / Stew'd in corruption, honeying and making love / Over thy nasty sty. . . ." The passage affects John "like the drums at the summer dances, if the drums could have spoken." He feels that it speaks directly to him and his situation, "about Linda lying there snoring, with the empty cup on the floor beside the bed; about Linda and Popé. . . ."

Episode 8: As John reads Shakespeare, he begins to hate Popé more and more, associating him with such Shakespearean villains as Iago and, above all, Claudius. He sees Shakespeare's words as magic, "and somehow it was as though he had never really hated Popé before; never really hated him because he had never been able to say how much he hated him." Literature is here endowed with the power to *create* emotion—John's reaction to Shakespeare is the perfect example of why literature is banned in London. When he reads of Hamlet's desire to murder Claudius, "when he is drunk asleep, or in his rage / Or in the incestuous pleasure of his bed," John is convinced that the words are telling him to kill Popé. He stabs Popé, who is lying "drunk asleep" in Linda's bed, but misses his mark and merely wounds him. Rather than beating John, however, Popé laughs at his tears and sends him out of the room, calling him "my brave Ahaiyuta."

Episode 9: John is 15, and Mitsima, an elder Indian, takes him to the river and teaches him how to work the clay into a traditional Indian pot. John's pot is messy and unusable, but he is incredibly happy to be included, even by one old man, in Indian tradition and education.

Episode 10: John, now 16, waits outside a house while a marriage ceremony takes place within. The bride and groom emerge and perform traditional Indian rituals, conducted by Mitsima. Linda scoffs at the ceremony, thinking that "it does seem a lot of fuss to make about so little." John, however, is profoundly affected and runs away from the crowd. He is heartbroken, for he is in love with the bride, Kiakimé. Of course, John is unable to speak of this to Linda, as it is yet another example of his "savagery" or her failure to properly condition him.

Episode 11: It is a special evening in the pueblo, for it is the night in which the young men perform the rituals that announce their manhood. Excited and nervous, John follows the Indian teens to the ladder leading into the Antelope Kiva, an underground cave in which the ritual takes place. Yet as he prepares to follow the others down into the kiva, he is stopped and struck by the observers, who yell, "Not for you, white-hair! Not for the son of the she-dog!" Amid a shower of stones, John runs out onto the mesa, where he stares off the edge of the precipice, contemplating suicide. He sees blood drip from a wound on his hand and thinks of *Macbeth*: "To-morrow and to-morrow and to-morrow. . . . [John] had discovered Time and Death and God." In other words, his solitude and learning eventually introduced John to the three things most feared by "civilized" society, foreshadowing his inability to exist in that world any better than he exists in the world of the Indians.

Bernard is struck by John's description of his loneliness and relates to him as an outsider in his society. John is surprised, citing Linda's descriptions of London, which revolve around the idea that no one is ever alone. Bernard blushingly explains, "I'm rather different from most people, I suppose. If one happens to be decanted different. . . ." John is quick to understand: "If one's different, one's bound to be lonely."

Bernard invites John and Linda to return to London with him and Lenina, "making the first move in a campaign whose strategy he had been secretly elaborating ever since, in the little house, he had realized who the 'father' of this young savage must be." Recall that John's father is the Director, the man planning to exile Bernard to Iceland. If Bernard can embarrass him by presenting his viviparous "son," then presumably he will gain the leverage needed to negotiate his position and remain in London. John, however, is unaware of this ulterior motive and is thrilled by the prospect of finally seeing the Other Place. He quotes Miranda from *The Tempest*, when she finally gets the opportunity to see mankind outside of her father on their small island: "O wonder! . . . How many goodly creatures are there here! How beauteous mankind is! . . . O brave new world that has such people in it." Bernard is perplexed by John's Shakespearean language, and the chapter ends with his reaction to the passage: "Hadn't you better wait till you actually see the new world?"

In **chapter 9**, Lenina returns to the hotel in Malpais after her "day of queerness and horror"; she treats herself to a dose of soma large enough to give her an 18-hour holiday. Bernard, on the other hand, lies awake all night perfecting his plan to bring John and Linda back to London. In the morning, while Lenina is still "on *soma*-holiday," he flies to Santa Fe and calls the World Controller's Office in London. After telling his story to several undersecretaries, Bernard is connected directly to Mustapha Mond, who asks Bernard to bring the two "savages" back as a matter of scientific interest. Feeling very important after speaking with a World Controller, Bernard obtains the necessary passes from the Warden and returns to Malpais before Lenina wakes up.

While Bernard is in Santa Fe, John approaches the hotel where Lenina and Bernard are staying. He was invited to visit them but receives no answer when he knocks at the door. Terrified that the two foreigners left without him (and upset because he thinks he will never again have the chance to see Lenina, on whom he has developed a substantial infatuation), John smashes a window and crawls into Lenina's room. He sees her luggage and is relieved to know that she has not yet left; he assumes that she is simply out of the hotel. He furtively rifles through her suitcase, delighting in civilized accoutrements such as her perfumed handkerchiefs, scented powder, and zippicamiknicks (apparently her undergarment). He is startled to hear a noise coming from the bedroom, and he hastily stuffs her possessions back in the suitcase and sneaks over to investigate the source of the noise. He finds Lenina, lying semiconscious on soma-holiday in her bed, wearing pink zippyjamas. John nearly cries with her beauty and is inspired to recite a passage from Shakespeare's *Troilus and Cressida*, in which Troilus obsesses over the seemingly supernatural whiteness of Cressida's hand; the passage reminds him of another Shakespearean passage, and he continues, whispering Romeo's adulation of Juliet's hand. Both passages concern the extreme purity of the heroine. By piling the significance of whiteness—virginity, purity, chastity—onto Lenina, John creates an image of her as the embodiment of all these things. Lenina, however, is neither virginal nor chaste, which has the potential to cause much friction between John's expectations of Lenina and Lenina herself.

John is interrupted by the sound of buzzing; the helicopter carrying Bernard is landing outside. He just has time to run from the room and through the open window before he meets Bernard, who is, of course, expecting him.

The narrative returns to London in **chapter 10**. In the Hatchery and Conditioning Centre, the Director and Henry Foster walk into the Fertilizing Room, where the Director has asked Bernard to meet them. He plans to publicly announce Bernard's exile, making an example of him. Henry points out that, for all of his eccentricities, Bernard still does his work quite well, prompting the Director to launch into a series of hypnopaedic axioms such as, "His intellectual eminence carries with it corresponding moral responsibilities" and "The greater a man's talents, the greater his power to lead astray." Therefore, although Bernard is a valuable worker, "unorthodoxy threatens more than the life of a mere individual; it strikes at Society itself," and "it is better that one should suffer than that many should be corrupted."

Bernard enters, and the Director asks for the attention of all the workers in the room and describes Bernard's flaws, from his heretical views on soma to the abnormality of his sex life. He concludes his harangue by sentencing Bernard to exile in Iceland, where he will be unable to corrupt innocent workers. More as a formality than anything else, the Director asks Bernard if he has anything to say in his defense. Bernard surprises him by bringing in Linda, who quite obscenely runs up to "her Tomakin," the Director, and hugs him desperately. Her appearance shocks everyone in the room; no one is accustomed or prepared to see the signs of old age and malnutrition. The Director is shocked, but the situation worsens exponentially when she reveals that she bore him a son after she was lost. John then enters, approaches the Director, kneels before him, and says, "My father!" Unlike the word "mother," which implies gross incorrectness and made the observers feel extremely uncomfortable, "father" is "a scatological rather than a pornographic impropriety." Gasps turn to hysterical laughter, and the Director flees the room in disgrace.

In **chapter 11**, Bernard's revelation of John and Linda causes a sensation in London. The Director resigns in humiliation, and John becomes a cross between a celebrity and novelty act. All of upper-caste London clamors to meet him, and his notoriety spills over to his guardian and chaperone, Bernard. Bernard no longer has difficulty convincing women to go out with him (a fact about which he brags to Helmholtz, causing a rift between them when Bernard accuses Helmholtz of jealousy), and his parties become the hottest ticket in town, for it is only through Bernard that one is able to meet "the savage."

London is less amused by Linda, a failure of conditioning rather than a true savage. Her grotesque appearance makes conditioned citizens physically ill. Furthermore, her being a "mother" is simply obscene, while John's "sonhood" is an interesting and forgivable (to an extent) eccentricity. Linda is not bothered by her ostracization, as she is thrilled with the newly available supply of soma. Greedy for endless holiday, she lies in a bedroom 24 hours a day, constantly taking higher doses of soma. Dr. Shaw admits that, at this rate of consumption, the soma will kill Linda in a matter of months. No one but John, however, see this as a problem, and even John is convinced that Linda will be happier living two months in bliss than years in unhappiness. Dr. Shaw explains that in a way, soma will actually *lengthen* Linda's life: "Every *soma*-holiday is a bit of what our ancestors used to call eternity."

Bernard escorts John around London, touring everything from the Weather Department's balloon in the sky to the

Electrical Equipment Corporation to Eton, the futuristic incarnation of England's prestigious boarding school. John is less than impressed. He finds the immense speed of the Bombay Green Rocket subpar in comparison to Shakespeare's Ariel, who "could put a girdle round the earth in forty minutes." Seeing masses of Bokanovsky Groups makes him physically sick, and he again recalls *The Tempest*, this time ironically remembering Miranda's excitement, "O brave new world that has such people in it." John's lack of excitement prompts Bernard to send a concerned letter to Mustapha Mond, in which he timidly admits to agreeing with some of John's ideas: "I must admit that I agree with the Savage in finding civilized infantility too easy or, as he put it, not expensive enough; and I would like to take this opportunity of drawing your fordship's attention to . . ." Bernard's self-importance evokes laughter from Mond, who thinks that one day he will have to teach Bernard a lesson about the social order.

Lenina, too, has become a bit of a celebrity due to her association with "the savage." She has been on dates with men as important as the Resident World Controller's Second Secretary and the Arch-Community-Songster of Canterbury. She confides to Fanny that much of the attention is due to the assumption that she has made love to John, which much to her disappointment and confusion, she has not. She is very attracted to him and often catches him staring at her, but he seems reluctant to admit that he finds her desirable.

The last part of the chapter follows Lenina on an evening with John (Bernard is going out on a date himself and asks Lenina to escort John to the Feelies). They go to see a Feely titled *Three Weeks in a Helicopter. An All-Super-Singing, Synthetic-Talking, Coloured, Stereoscopic Feely with Synchronized Scent-Organ Accompaniment.* The story is that of a black man whose conditioning is wiped from his brain after a helicopter accident. He falls madly in love with a Beta-Plus blonde, kidnaps her, and holds her captive in his helicopter for three weeks. She is rescued finally by three men, who send the man off to an Adult Re-Conditioning Centre (apparently this new society is prepared for incidents in which conditioning fails) and take the blonde as a mistress. Thus it ends conventionally. John is aroused by the show and desperately desires Lenina, who obviously expects him to stay the night in her apartment. He is ashamed of his desire and refuses to look too long at Lenina, "obscurely terrified lest she should cease to be something he could feel himself worthy of. . . . 'I don't think you ought to see things like that,' he said, making haste to transfer from Lenina herself to the surrounding circumstances the blame for any past or possible future lapse from perfection." Lenina is confused by John's condemnation of what she thought was a "lovely" film. She attempts to persuade him to come into her apartment when the taxicopter arrives, but he quickly tells her goodnight and flies away. He hurries home, where he desperately rereads *Othello*, comparing the plot to that of *Three Weeks in a Helicopter*. Lenina copes with her disappointment by taking an extra half-gram of soma.

Bernard is having another of his parties in **chapter 12**, this one particularly prestigious because the Arch-Community-Songster of Canterbury has accepted the invitation. John yells at Bernard for not asking whether or not he wanted to have another party in his honor and refuses to leave his locked room. Instead, he sits in solitude and reads *Romeo and Juliet*.

Bernard pleads with John to leave his bedroom and come down to the party, but John has lost interest in being a novelty. Humiliated, Bernard announces that the guest of honor will not appear. His guests are quite angry, abandoning their politeness toward Bernard, "furious at having been tricked into behaving politely to this insignificant fellow with the unsavoury reputation and the heretical opinions." Bernard's short-lived celebrity is over.

Lenina accompanied the Arch-Songster to the party and is particularly upset at John's absence. Still confused about his actions during their evening at the Feelies, she had decided to confess to him that she liked him more than she had ever liked another man. She assumes that his refusal to appear is because he does not like her and does not want to see her. She "felt all the sensations normally experienced at the beginning of a Violent Passion Surrogate treatment—a sense of dreadful emptiness, a breathless apprehension, a nausea. Her heart seemed to stop beating." Against all of her conditioning, Lenina seems to be experiencing emotion. Like Bernard and Helmholtz Watson, she is treading the line between behavior that is acceptable to conditioned society and that which is strictly forbidden.

The narrative skips to the office of Mustapha Mond, who reads a paper titled "A New Theory of Biology." Mond acts as censor, reading new material such as this paper and then deciding whether it is suitable for publication. He deems this paper "*Not to be published*," reflecting that "it was a masterly piece of work. But once you began admitting explanations in terms of purpose—well, you didn't know what the result might be." Mond worries that this paper, and others like it, has the potential to "upset some of the unsettled minds" in London's upper caste and spark ideas that "the purpose of life was not the maintenance of well-being, but some enlargement of knowledge. Which was, the Controller reflected, quite possibly true. But not, in the present circumstances, admissible." While John's appearance in London seems to be bringing out heretical elements in good citizens like Lenina, "uncivilized" elements already exist in the society, and they exist in the minds of the most powerful. Some people, such as Mond, realize that conditioning is not a moral decision but a practical one and that it does come with a price—new ideas and progress.

Huxley takes us back to Bernard's room, where he weeps in his humiliation after all of his guests leave. Unlike the Bernard from the first half of the novel, he copes with his despair by taking soma and going to sleep. The following day, he gets sympathy from both John and Helmholtz, who forgives him for abandoning their friendship during his brief celebrity. Bernard, however, is both grateful to and resentful of both men and is overwhelmingly jealous that the two of them immediately become friends. Helmholtz has recently been in a bit of trouble with "Authority" as the result of reading to his students a rhyme he had written about the joys of solitude. He reads the poem to John, who in turn pulls out his copy of *The Complete Works of William Shakespeare* and reads to Helmholtz. The two men begin to meet regularly, delighting in finding another who appreciates the writings of Shakespeare. They are always accompanied by Bernard, who does not understand their fascination with the forbidden author and takes every opportunity to interrupt the recitations and make fun of them.

Helmholtz loves listening to Shakespeare's words, and the reader is reminded of his earlier feeling that he could write something more meaningful if only he had something to write about. Shakespeare's plots, while sometimes a bit "ridiculous" and "mad," show Helmholtz the sorts of situations that inspire meaningful composition. When John begins reading *Romeo and Juliet*, however, Helmholtz is unable to step outside of his conditioning enough to become engrossed in the play. He laughs hysterically when Juliet threatens suicide if she is forced to marry Paris; he cannot understand the concept of monogamous love. John is offended by Helmholtz's disrespect for the story, for he sees it as an analogy for his relationship with Lenina. He locks the book back up in its drawer "with the gesture of one who removes his pearl from before swine." Helmholtz apologizes, explaining, "You can't expect me to keep a straight face about fathers and mothers. And who's going to get excited about a boy having a girl or not having her?" Helmholtz reads Shakespeare as an outline—a method of teaching himself how to compose something meaningful. He is disappointed in *Romeo and Juliet* because it is too unrealistic for him: "No . . . it won't do. We need some other kind of madness and violence."

In **chapter 13**, Lenina is at work in the Embryo Store when Henry Foster asks her to accompany him to a Feely. She declines, and Henry notes "weariness," "pallor," and "sadness" in her face. "Afraid that she might be suffering from one of the few remaining infectious diseases," he suggests she visit a doctor and have a Pregnancy Substitute or a Violent Passion Surrogate (V.P.S.). Lenina is irritated by this last suggestion: "She would have laughed, if she hadn't been on the point of crying. As though she hadn't got enough V. P. of her own." Thinking of John, she is so distracted that she loses track of which bottles she has already immunized with a sleeping sickness vaccination. This utopian, perfectly immunized society is still subject to human error, and Lenina's mistake will cause a young Alpha Minus to die of the disease, "the first case for over half a century."

Fanny is shocked by Lenina's unhealthy obsession with a single man. She first attempts to convince Lenina that there is no reason to focus on only one man (recall her conversation with Lenina in chapter 3 regarding Lenina's potential monogamy with Henry). When Lenina insists that she can't stop thinking of John, Fanny changes tactics, seeing Lenina's obsession as the result of John's refusal to "be had." She tells Lenina to simply "go and take him . . . whether he wants it or no."

Inspired by Fanny's firmness, Lenina doses herself on soma and goes to John's apartment that evening. She reproaches John for not being more excited to see her, and he responds by falling to his knees and confessing his love for her. Unable to express his feelings using his own words (words concerning "love" had never been taught to him, for not only are they socially unacceptable, but by A.F. 632, no one knows them), he falls back to Shakespeare, reciting Ferdinand's declarations of love to Miranda in *The Tempest*. He abruptly pulls away, however, as Lenina leans in to kiss him, telling her he needs to perform some sort of difficult task in order to be worthy of her. Lenina is annoyed, and John tries to explain: "At Malpais, you had to bring her the skin of a mountain lion—I mean, when you wanted to marry some one." Lenina snaps, "There aren't any lions in England." They argue, Lenina trying to make John act sensibly (i.e., give in and sleep with her), and John desperately trying to make Lenina understand his idea of romance. Lenina is finally exasperated when John starts talking about marriage and fidelity; she interrupts him and reduces everything down to a simple question: Does he or doesn't he like her? John admits that he loves her "more than anything in the world," giving Lenina some relief and allowing her to embrace him. Lenina, despite John's explanations about chastity and fidelity, still sees attraction as the bottom line in the discussion—if John likes her and she likes him, there is no more to discuss. She begins to undress, prompting John to turn from

Ferdinand's avowals of love to Othello's accusations of infidelity. Reacting as much to his own desire as to Lenina's sexual behavior, he calls her a whore and an "impudent strumpet," pushing her away from him and hitting her. Terrified, she flees to his bathroom and locks herself in, begging John to slide her clothes over the door. He paces in the other room, reciting bits of *King Lear*, *Othello*, and *Troilus and Cressida* that revolve around the weakness and impurity of women. He is interrupted by a telephone call informing him that Linda has taken ill and was moved to the Park Lane Hospital for the Dying. Forgetting about Lenina in the bathroom, he rushes from the apartment, leaving Lenina to sneak out, confused and still terrified by John's scathing verbal and physical abuse.

At the Park Lane Hospital for the Dying in **chapter 14**, John is escorted to Ward 81, where Linda lies, sliding in and out of consciousness, in Bed 20. The ward is full, but Linda is the only person who shows any signs of age; progress has been such that old age descends rapidly and kills a person before he or she shows any external signs of aging. The nurse explains to John that they try to make the hospital "something between a first-class hotel and a feely-palace"; scent and sound are kept constantly flowing through the room, and televisions are always on. John sits beside Linda's bed, crying as he remembers her, young and pretty, singing lullabies to him when he was a baby, teaching him to read as he got older, and, most clearly, her telling him stories about London, "that beautiful, beautiful Other Place, whose memory, as of heaven, a paradise of goodness and loveliness, he still kept whole and intact, undefiled by contact with the reality of this real London, these actual civilized men and women."

John's tears and memories are interrupted by the entrance of a Bokanovsky group of eight-year-old Delta boys. They run through the ward as though it is their playground but stop short at the sight of Linda, confused by her appearance. John is shocked and angered by their presence and insensitivity, and he slaps one, bringing the Head Nurse running. She threatens to throw John from the ward if he continues to interfere with the children's "death-conditioning." Interaction with the grieving and angry John would set back the children, who are slowly and consistently conditioned to associate death and the Hospital for the Dying with ice cream and fun. The nurse lures the children away from Bed 20 with promises of chocolate eclairs.

Distracted and upset, John is unable to recall his pleasant memories of Linda from minutes before. He can now only remember images of her drunk, in bed with Popé, and being shouted at by the other boys in the pueblo. He leans toward her, desperate for her to recognize him and understand the significance of the moment, but she is lost in a soma-haze and calls him Popé. John squeezes her hand, trying to "force her to come back from this dream of ignoble pleasures . . . back into the present, back into reality; the appalling present, the awful reality—but sublime, but significant, but desperately important precisely because of the imminence of that which made them so fearful." John wants Linda to acknowledge her fear of death; he does not realize this is impossible, as Linda has been conditioned, just like the children running through the ward, to see death as something natural and perhaps even lovely.

Linda reacts to his touch, again calling him Popé. Angered at her delusion and drugged acceptance of her impending death, John shakes her violently. Linda wakes up for a moment and recognizes him, but she then begins to choke, no longer able to take a breath. Panicked, John runs down the ward, calling for the nurse; by the time they reach the bed, Linda is dead. John falls to his knees and sobs uncontrollably, distressing the nurse, who again worries about the possible damage to the children's conditioning. She leads them away from the mourning man, but a few boys slip away from her and stay behind. They stare curiously at Linda and at John, asking innocently and smilingly if she is dead. John pushes them away and silently leaves the hospital.

In **chapter 15**, John leaves the Park Lane Hospital for the Dying at six o'clock, shift change for the Delta menial staff. He exits the elevator into a sea of Deltas, two Bokanovsky Groups clamoring for the daily ration of soma. John is always nauseated by the sight of so many identical twins, but today, leaving the deathbed of his mother, their existence seems offensive and mocking: "Like maggots they had swarmed defilingly over the mystery of Linda's death . . . they now crawled across his grief and his repentance." Miranda's words come to him yet again; "Now, suddenly, they trumpeted a call to arms. 'O brave new world!' Miranda was proclaiming the possibility of transforming even the nightmare into something fine and noble. 'O brave new world!' It was a challenge, a command." The words inspire John, and he is struck by the need for liberty: "Linda had been a slave, Linda had died; others should live in freedom, and the world be made beautiful." John pushes his way through the crowd of Deltas, screaming, "Stop! . . . Listen, I beg of you. . . . Lend me your ears. . . . Don't take that horrible stuff. It's poison . . ." The Deltas are confused and angry at the suggestion that they will not receive their usual dose of soma; John continues shouting at them to "throw it all away. . . . I come to bring you freedom." The Deputy Sub-Bursar, the authority over the crowd of Deltas and the distributor of soma, scampers to a telephone.

Back in Helmholtz's apartment, he and Bernard wonder where John could be. They are about to leave for dinner without him when Helmholtz receives a telephone call from a friend at the Park Lane Hospital for the Dying, presumably the Deputy Sub-Bursar, telling him that John has apparently gone crazy. He and Bernard rush there, arriving in time to hear John calling the uncomprehending Deltas "mewling and puking babies." He grabs the box full of soma and, to the distress of the mob, begins throwing pillboxes out the window. The mob rushes forward, and while Bernard fearfully looks away, Helmholtz runs toward John, joining in his shouts for freedom. Bernard watches in indecision as his two friends fight the crowd, but he cannot muster the bravery to help them. His "agony of humiliated indecision" is ended when the police arrive, armed with tanks of soma-vapour, hoses of water-based anaesthetic, and a portable Synthetic Music Box playing the "Voice of Reason" and the "Voice of Good Feeling," pathetically pleading with the mob to cease their violence and love one another again. These weapons effectively quell the riot, causing the Deltas, and even John and Helmholtz, to stop fighting and instead hug one another. The Deltas are quickly given fresh pillboxes of soma, and the police lead away John, Helmholtz, and Bernard, who protests his arrest and unsuccessfully attempts to deny his friendship with "the Savage."

In **chapter 16**, John, Helmholtz, and Bernard have been brought to Mustapha Mond's study, where they wait for him: John disinterestedly browses through the room, Helmholtz is strangely cheerful, and Bernard is terrified and silent. Mond enters and good-humoredly questions John, who admits (much to Bernard's horror) that he does not care much for "civilization." He does, however, appreciate the constant music, a comment to which the Controller responds with, "Sometimes a thousand twangling instruments will hum about my ears and sometimes voices." John is surprised and delighted by Mond's knowledge of *The Tempest*, saying, "I thought nobody knew about that book here, in England." Mond divulges that he, as a lawmaker, has the power to break the laws banning literature. John (now referred to almost exclusively as "the savage") confesses that he does not understand the reason behind banning Shakespeare, prompting Mond to lecture him in the dangers of anything old and beautiful: "Beauty's attractive, and we don't want people to be attracted by old things. We want them to like new ones." He admits that *Othello* is more beautiful than *Three Weeks in a Helicopter* but points out that not only would *Othello* be subversive to this consumer-based, passionless society, but society would be unable to appreciate the beauty of the play anyway (John remembers Helmholtz's reaction to Juliet's passions and cannot help but agree). Helmholtz interrupts, saying that he desires to write something as beautiful as Shakespeare but with a story to which modern, conditioned humans could relate. Mond responds, "And it's what you will never write. . . . Because if it were really like *Othello* nobody could understand it, however new it might be. And if it were new, it couldn't possibly be like *Othello*. . . . Because our world is not the same as Othello's world. You can't make flivvers without steel—and you can't make tragedies without social instability. The world's stable now."

Mond sympathizes with John and Helmholtz but contends that stability and happiness (modern happiness, not Shakespeare's "overcompensations for misery") are worth the price of high art and science. Helmholtz is shocked by the inclusion of science in this statement, pointing out that everyone is conditioned to believe that "science is everything." Mond, however, speaks of his own duty to censor any scientific thought that might alter society in any way, for "every change is a menace to stability." He admits that in his youth he worked as a physicist and was good enough to "realize that all our science is just a cookery book, with an orthodox theory of cooking that nobody's allowed to question, and a list of recipes that mustn't be added to except by special permission from the head cook." Mond's own experiments apparently toed the line between acceptable and heretical science, and he was finally given the choice between being exiled to an island or becoming a World Controller and giving up his own scientific quest for the truth in exchange for the power to keep the masses stable and happy. Obviously, he chose the second option, but he admits that at times he wonders whether he would have been happier on an island after all, where he could have met the most interesting set of men and women to be found anywhere in the world. All the people who, for one reason or another, have got too "self-consciously individual to fit into community-life." In fact, the Controller acknowledges that a part of him envies Helmholtz for his impending exile.

This talk of exile proves too much for Bernard, who becomes hysterical and has to be subdued (with soma) and carried to another room by four of Mond's secretaries. Helmholtz, however, is excited at the prospect of living on an island, having the freedom to pursue individual ideas and associate with others who have not been totally shaped by their conditioning. Mond offers him a choice of islands, suggesting that perhaps he would prefer a tropical or mild island. Sounding more like John than a civilized Londoner, Helmholtz answers: "I should like a thoroughly bad climate. . . . I believe one would write better if the climate were bad. If there were a lot of wind and storms, for example. . . ." Helmholtz will be exiled to the Falkland Islands.

Dignified and inspired in the face of his impending exile, Helmholtz leaves Mond's study to check on Bernard in **chapter 17**. John and Mond are finally alone, and Huxley indulges in a debate between their two positions—viviparous versus engineered life—disguised as a conversation.

Still smarting from his mother's death, and completely disillusioned with the "brave new world," John bitingly reminds the Controller that stability and continuous happiness come with the price tag of art and science. Mond agrees with John and perhaps a bit nostalgically mentions that religion must also be abandoned. Mond attempts to explain the concept of God to the savage but soon realizes that John probably understands God and religion better than he, as he grew up on a Reservation where worship was central to the community (recall John's devastation when he is not allowed to undergo the mystical coming-of-age ritual with the other boys). Mond's knowledge comes from literary artifacts; in his safe there is a well-worn copy of the Holy Bible, as well as copies of other religious texts and theological treatises. Mond laughs: "A whole collection of pornographic old books. God in the safe and Ford on the shelves." John is appalled that Mond has the knowledge of God (which John seems to believe is the ultimate unquestionable) but withholds it from the populace, a position Mond is quick to defend. He explains that, as with *Othello*, the world would not understand the Bible, that it concerns "God hundreds of years ago. Not about God now. . . . Men [change]." Mond attempts to explain with the writings of Cardinal Newman and Maine de Biran (*Cardinal* and *philosopher* being terms John can define only using quotations from Shakespeare). Newman argues that "independence was not made for man—that it is an unnatural state—will do for a while, but will not carry us on safely to the end," while Maine suggests that "the religious sentiment tends to develop as we grow older; to develop because, as the passions grow calm, as the fancy and sensibilities are less excited and excitable, our reason becomes less troubled in its working, less obscured by the images, desires and distractions, in which it used to be absorbed." Mond uses these arguments to justify why religion would be out of place in the modern world, where there *is* no old age, no passions to dim, and no excitable youth to entertain the idea of independent existence. There is simply no basis for religious belief in A.F. 632. Mond punctuates this by admitting that he believes there is a God: "[now] he manifests himself as an absence."

John valiantly attempts to find an argument for the introduction of religion into this world of eugenics and mind-control, but Mond counters him at every point. God would allow man a reason for "bearing things patiently"; but now there is nothing to bear. God would give a reason for self-denial; but "industrial civilization is only possible when there's no self-denial." God would be a reason for chastity; but stability would crumble under the weight of passion that chastity would introduce. God would be the reason for heroism and nobility of soul; but heroism and virtue thrive on conflict, and without wars there need be no heroes.

Nearly defeated, John finally quotes *Hamlet*: "What you need is something *with* tears for a change. Nothing costs enough here. . . . Exposing what is mortal and unsure to all that fortune, death and danger dare, even for an eggshell. Isn't there something in that? . . . Quite apart from God—though of course God would be a reason for it. Isn't there something in living dangerously?" Mond quickly agrees, yes there is an enormous benefit to the rush of adrenaline; hence the mandatory monthly Violent Passion Surrogate, which physically simulates the effects of all of the passion eliminated by soma and conditioning. "All the tonic effects of murdering Desdemona and being murdered by Othello, without any of the inconveniences."

John insists that he craves the inconveniences: "I don't want comfort. I want God, I want poetry, I want real danger, I want freedom, I want goodness. I want sin." Mond reminds him that with these things, he is also stuck with old age, disease, starvation, fear, torture, and a multitude of other horrors. "I claim them all" is John's only response. There is no further argument; the savage and the Controller understand each other, but ultimately they disagree at the heart of the issue. John wants to make the decision Mond chose not to so many years ago; he wants individuality instead of stability.

In **chapter 18**, Helmholtz and Bernard visit John to say their farewells. They are surprised to find him vomiting, the result of a "purification ritual he has imposed on himself, drinking mustard mixed with warm water." Astonished, they ask if he ate something rancid; he replies: "I ate civilization . . . It poisoned me; I was defiled. And then . . . I ate my own wickedness." In the face of his approaching exile, Bernard has regained some of his self-respect and bravely apologizes to John for his behavior at the party. John and Helmholtz silence him; the situation has allied the three of them beyond what now seem like insignificant personal spats. John tells the two men that he asked to be sent to the Falkland Islands with them, but that the Controller refused, saying "he wanted to go on with the experiment." John is furious as he recounts the decision, asserting that he refuses to "experimented with" and shall run away "anywhere . . . so long as I can be alone."

The chapter skips forward an unspecified amount of time (not too long, presumably), and John has fled London. He decides to take up hiding in an abandoned lighthouse only 15 minutes by air to London but sufficiently isolated since it was no longer near the fields of any country games, so completely removed from the life of nature-hating population. Before he sleeps in the lighthouse, he spends a night purifying himself (by prayer and voluntary crucifixion, much as he described to Bernard soon after they met) so that he is worthy of the "almost too comfortable" ferro-concrete structure. He intends to spend the rest of his life in total solitude, living off a garden (he brought seeds with him) and wild game; one of his first chores is constructing a bow and arrows out of a nearby ash tree. Note Huxley's choice of tree: The ash is identified in mythologies from many cultures, including Norse and Greek. Its sweet manna is often recognized as a (sometimes) supernatural intoxicant and sometimes is even referred to as "soma." While whittling ash branches for a bow, John realizes that he is singing to himself, and in punishment for his enjoyment, he mixes his mustard water to purge. Following this internal purification,

John fashions a whip out of knotted cords and beats himself to the point of drawing blood and beyond. Unfortunately, this display was witnessed by three Delta Minuses, who were inexplicably driving instead of taking public transportation. They are shocked and rush off, but John's isolation is over.

Three days after John's unwitting display, reporters descend on his lighthouse, anxious to interview him. Not surprisingly, John kicks a reporter, prompting the others to maintain a certain distance, but this does not discourage them from harassing him from afar. He finally shoots a homemade arrow into a hovering helicopter and is seemingly left alone.

It is not long before John finds another excuse to whip himself into purification; this time he is appalled by lustful thoughts of Lenina, whom he last saw naked and willing in his apartment before he screamed at her in rage and frightened her into taking refuge in his bathroom. John does not realize that an "expert big game photographer" had been camping out near the lighthouse for three days, laying microphones, wires, and cameras in the hope that John would put on another savage display. He captures John's entire self-inflicted punishment on film, and it is released as a Feely a mere 12 days later—*The Savage of Surrey*. The popularity of the real-life footage prompts a renewed interest in John's savage lifestyle, and his property is swarmed by workers desperate to catch a glimpse of the Savage beating himself in a frenzy. They ignore his shouts, delighting in his anger as he begs them to leave, ecstatic when he picks up the now-famous whip and waves it threateningly (there is, however, nothing he can really do against so many). The circus is interrupted by the arrival of Lenina (accompanied by Henry Foster), who steps toward John with her arms open as though to embrace him. He snaps and rushes at her, screaming "Strumpet" and "Fitchew," as usual relying on Shakespeare to vent his most passionate feelings. The mob shrieks, "Let's see the whipping stunt" and is rapturous as John begins to whip Lenina; they close in tighter, desperate to touch the Savage and witness his wildness firsthand. John turns the whip on his own body, shouting, "Oh, the flesh! Kill it, kill it!"

"Drawn by the fascination of the horror of pain, from within, impelled by that habit of cooperation, that desire for unanimity and atonement, which their conditioning had so ineradicably implanted in them, they began to mime the frenzy of his gestures, striking at one another as the Savage struck at his own rebellious flesh, or at that plump incarnation of turpitude writhing in the heather at his feet." As the mob attacks itself, someone sings "Orgy-Porgy," and what had been a violent frenzy morphs into a religious/sexual Solidarity Song.

Caught up in the orgy, John is also swept along in a soma-induced passion. After midnight, the mob finally disperses, leaving John to sleep off his "long-drawn frenzy of sexuality." He wakes, alone, the following morning and is shamed by the memory of his loss of control.

Reporters, desperate for more information about the previous night's "orgy of atonement" (as it was dubbed by the press), descend on the lighthouse that afternoon. John is nowhere to be seen, and they enter the building. There they discover his body, dangling slowly back and forth, as it hangs from the second floor. John has lost his loss of control, which he views has a loss of principle, morals, and most importantly, discipline. He has tasted soma and engaged in the most sacred of Fordian customs (the orgy/impromptu Solidarity Service), and he seems to have enjoyed it. But this behavior, and especially the enjoyment of this behavior, is unacceptable to John's unconditioned mind, and perhaps finally realizing the hopelessness of his situation—that he is neither a member of London society or the Reservation—John commits suicide.

Critical Views

RUDOLF B. SCHMERL ON CREATING FANTASY

Aldous Huxley's *Brave New World* is generally recognized as one of the two most widely discussed English fantasies of this century. The other, of course, is Orwell's *1984*. The two books seem to present the two plausible alternative directions totalitarianism may take. . . .

Fantasy may be defined as the deliberate presentation of improbabilities through any one of four methods—the use of unverifiable time, place, characters, or devices—to a typical reader within a culture whose level of sophistication will enable that reader to recognize the improbabilities. *Brave New World* employs two of the methods of fantasy, unverifiable time and devices[.] . . .

The choice of time rather than space as the method through which a fantasy achieves its distance from reality confronts the fantasist with a problem the alternate choice avoids. A reader does not require an explanation of the origin of the differences between Lilliput and London or Mars and Los Angeles. The fantasist can rely on the common observation that what is far away is likely to be different, and no one will ask pedantic questions about the evolution of Martian species. But what is far away in time is something else again. Time is almost always used in a forward direction by a fantasist (to go backwards, unless he goes back very far indeed, means to wrestle with the quite different problems of the historical novel), and the gap between the present and that point in the future at which the fantasy begins is not at all like the spatial gap between London and Lilliput or Los Angeles and Mars. Between London and Lilliput there is a great deal of water, and between Los Angeles and Mars, a great deal of space, and neither ocean necessitates explication.[1] But what is between 1932 A.D. (when *Brave New World* was published) and 632 A.F. (when the fantasy begins)? The opening three chapters of *Brave New World* are designed to answer this question while simultaneously setting the stage for what is to follow.

Huxley's technique in these opening chapters has been described both as poetic[2] and dramatic,[3] largely because Mustapha's lecture to the students is intermixed with bits of dialogue and internal monologue on the part of various staff members of the Central London Hatchery and Conditioning Centre, as well as with scenes, past and present, which illustrate what is being talked about. There is another way, however, to regard Huxley's technique here, and that is as fantastic historiography. All the action of the first chapter takes place in the Fertilizing Room, the Bottling Room, the Embryo Store, and the Social Predestination Room of the Hatchery and Conditioning Centre—and in that order. When the Director of the Hatchery tells the students that he will "begin at the beginning,"[4] Huxley chooses not only the logical start for the Director's lecture but also the logical beginning of an account of the society of the brave new world. Huxley begins, in other words, with biology, and with the very beginnings of biology at that. But he describes no more than is relevant to his theme: the first chapter ends as the students are on their way to the Decanting Room, and the second chapter opens as they go to the Neo-Pavlovian Conditioning Rooms of the Infant Nurseries. The Decanting Room represents a biological technicality not really germane to an introduction to the World State, and is thus properly left in the void between the first two chapters.

The theme of the first chapter is the biological foundation of the World State; the theme of the second, the psychological super-structure erected on that foundation. In the Director's account of the reasons for, and the practice of, hypnopaedic indoctrination, Huxley begins to interweave historical flashbacks. The suggestion is that these flashbacks are evoked in the students' minds by the Director's lecture, for Huxley has been moving back and forth from the Director's speech to the students' minds since they first entered the Fertilizing Room. But Huxley is also addressing the reader directly. The Director, Huxley writes, "had a long chin and big, rather prominent teeth, just covered, when he was not talking, by his full, floridly curved lips. Old, young? Thirty? Fifty? Fifty-five? It was hard to say. And anyhow the question didn't arise; in this year of stability, A.F. 632, it didn't occur to you to ask it" (p. 3). That is the sentence with which Huxley announces he is writing a fantasy. It is not until the third chapter, when the Director's place is taken by Mustapha Mond, that Huxley begins to shift his own role from that of alternate narrator to that of the more impersonal recorder of dialogue and scene.[5]

Although the third chapter is one of the most unconventional stylistic pieces to be found in any of Huxley's novels—dialogue between various characters in different locations at the Hatchery is juxtaposed and intertwined to create a steadily increasing irony—it is, of the three opening chapters of the novel, the most conventional as history. Mustapha begins, like the Director, at the beginning, but this time the beginning is a matter of chronology. "You all remember," he says to the students, "that beautiful and inspired saying of Our Ford's: History is bunk" (p. 38). And in the following paragraph, all history preceding the time of Our Ford is swept away, history of which the students could know nothing, and is thus swept away only from the reader. Mustapha's account of the origin and development of the World State is Huxley's history of the future, taking the reader back to the present and then gradually bringing him forward again to the time at which the action of the fantasy begins. The story of Bernard Marx and John the Savage can thus be told against the background provided by the first three chapters, which means that the affair of John and Lenina is dramatically ironic in the traditional way: the reader knows more than the protagonist.

The use of unverifiable time in *Brave New World* is excessively complicated by the character of John. Bernard Marx and Helmholtz Watson could not have been enlarged into full-scale antagonists of their society without violating the conception of the novel; to suggest, however faintly, that something there is that does not love a brave new world, something inherent, that is, in protoplasm, transmitted through genes despite bottles and hypnopaedia, would imply an optimism totally inconsistent with Huxley's purpose. John is needed, then; he is the traveler in Utopia, the alien between whom and the natives no true understanding is possible, a Brobdingnagian among Gullivers. But in making John a strange mixture of Zuni Indian and Shakespearean tragic hero, Huxley introduces complications that blur the implicit comparison between 1932 and 632 A.F. Whatever Huxley gains by contrasting Shakespeare with the "feelies," genuine sexual passion with random promiscuity, a sense of guilt and honor with a sense of discomfort, he also loses by forcing the reader to look back three hundred years for values to set against the aesthetic and ethical vacuum of six hundred years in the future. Not only is the reader given too many temporal periods for simultaneous contemplation; there is also the implication that the brave new world already exists, at least in essence, in 1932: that, to gauge the emptiness of the World State, we must go to the fullness of Elizabethan times or to that of a savage culture. If the implication were accepted, there would hardly be much point in reading the book—let alone writing it.

Notes

1. With space, of course, there is the problem of traveling through it; that is, the fantasist has some obligation to account for whatever magical machine transports his characters to Mars and back again. An acute distinction between skilled and clumsy ways of doing this is made by Fletcher Pratt in his essay, "A Critique of Science Fiction," in Reginald Bretnor (ed.), *Modern Science Fiction* (New York: Coward McCann, 1953), pp. 74–90.

2. See Alexander Henderson, *Aldous Huxley* (London: Chatto and Windus, 1935).

3. Richard Gerber, *Utopian Fantasy* (London: Routledge and Began Paul, Ltd.), 1955), p. 125.

4. *Brave New World* (Garden City: Doubleday, Doran & Co., Inc., 1932), p. 3.

5. Once, later, Huxley interrupts to glance ahead, introducing an irrelevancy purely for the fun of it: Lenina forgets to give an embryo its sleeping sickness injection, and "twenty-two years, eight months, and four days from that moment, a promising young Alpha-Minus administrator at Mwanza-Mwanza was to die of trypanosomiasis—the first case for over half a century. Sighing, Lenina went on with her work" (p. 223).

In *Brave New World*, Aldous Huxley presents a global society entirely dependent on biotechnology. In this world, the pleasure principle reigns, and fetal chemical interference combined with infant sleep-conditioning dictate social strata (through a cloning process that has replaced pregnancy and childbirth). The opening passage's tour of the Central London Hatchery and Conditioning Centre explains the genetic manipulation that creates the different social classes, the encouraged use of *soma* (a recreational drug), the governmental and social promotion of promiscuity and sexual games, and the complex athletic activities that occupy adults in Huxley's entertainment-focused world.

The genders appear equal within the social order; both men and women work at the same jobs, have equal choice in sexual partners, and participate in the same leisure pursuits. Yet the system seems flawed when genetic manipulation errs, as in Bernard's case, or when we compare this "utopia" to life on the Reservation, which has preserved familial structure and has produced John, whose education via a volume of Shakespeare reflects more traditional expectations of gendered behavior. While Huxley acknowledges the advantages of a world free from disease, hunger, and class discontent, he questions the moral emptiness of a materialistic, sexually charged society that devalues individuals through its enforced focus on entertainment and its prohibition of close personal relationships between men and women. The novel reinforces traditional gender norms by inciting readers' disgust at the vacuous Lenina, whose sexual promiscuity and social freedom horrifies John (the Savage) and frustrates Bernard, the novel's "enlightened" characters.

Bernard chafes against the social system, particularly the sexual structure that denies him a monogamous relationship with Lenina. His relative introversion, caused by a suspected fetal chemical imbalance, allows him to step outside of the system and criticize it. He objects to his colleagues' discussion of Lenina's sexual enthusiasm, for example, thinking that they talk "about her as though she were a bit of meat" (38). Although he seizes the opportunity to strike out against the system by bringing John back from the Reservation, he falters when presented with the option of actually fighting back. When the Controller transfers him to an island for individually minded citizens, a terrified Bernard is literally dragged away.

While Bernard struggles and then succumbs, John suffers the most from the upheaval of traditional gender roles. He lusts after Lenina, couching his desire in romantic turns of phrase from his Shakespearean education. Yet he also sees her promiscuity as threatening and immoral, disallowing him the opportunity for an exclusive sexual relationship. Frustrated in his attempts to find a middle ground between his perceptions of honor and chivalry and his sexual desire, he unsuccessfully retreats from the society and eventually commits suicide.

Lenina represents the "brave new" womanhood of Huxley's world. She indulges in all the government-endorsed pursuits, although she is less sexually active than her friends and co-workers would like. Her initial leanings toward sexual monogamy leave her open to Bernard's advances, but her awkward encounters with John send her speedily back to the comforts of *soma* and promiscuity. Her seeming superficiality facilitates Huxley's warnings about the impact of mass consumerism and sexual liberty—she acts out the familiar "dumb blonde" stereotype. Yet Lenina also fulfills many goals for liberated women—she chooses sexual partners, is not trapped in a domestic role, has a successful career, and need not fear pregnancy and abandonment due to effective birth control. Lenina strikingly contrasts to Linda, John's mother, whose life on the Reservation has left her unattractive and desperately unhappy. Students might consider the ways in which Lenina and Linda represent the positive and negative impacts each social structure has on women's lives.

While describing the cloning process and birth control that have rendered pregnancy obsolete, Huxley explains the elimination of the concept of "mother" and "motherhood." Whereas procreation was once encouraged and "sacred," now mass sexual activity has become permissible. Words such as "baby" and "mother" are unmentionable, eliciting shock and horror. As June Deery and Deanna Madden explain, this replacement of procreation with sexual activity both liberates and confines women. Women are no longer tied to the household or seen as life vessels, nor are they repositories of family ideas in a non-familial world. Yet they are no longer valued for the same reasons. Bernard's feeling that his colleagues, and Lenina herself, think of her as a piece of meat indicates this devaluation. In addition, the abolition of motherhood allows the patriarchy of Ford's system to run unchecked without family needs displacing community affiliations. Although the genders are equal, no women occupy leadership positions—the men such as the Controller lead, usurping the guiding maternal hand and replacing it with paternal authority.

Robert L. Mack on Elements of Parody in *Brave New World*

The opening chapters of Huxley's novel memorably outline the conditions of life in the technologically controlled world of London in the year AF (After Ford) 632. Six centuries after the American individualist Henry Ford revolutionized the world with his advocacy of assembly-line mass production and thus, Huxley suggests, paved the way for a new era in secular civilization, the reader accompanies a group of young students on a tour of the Central London Hatchery and Conditioning Centre. The guide—scientist Henry Foster—explains the methods by which the embryos of the future are routinely and artificially fertilized, bottled, and finally 'decanted' into life. In the infant nurseries, the children are subjected to a process of lifelong conditioning to perform the ideal tasks for the class in society for which they have been created or 'predestined'; they are brainwashed into an unquestioning acceptance of the state motto: Community, Identity, Stability. Any form of individual personality or ability in Huxley's brave new world of the future, it would appear, is a thing of the past.

Into this world of mass production and neo-Pavlovian conditioning, Huxley introduces the character of John Savage—a young man who had been conventionally conceived, born, and raised in the primitive society of a New Mexican 'Savage Reservation', and whose primary source of education from his twelfth year has been 'a thick book' with 'loose and crumpled' pages—the *Complete Works of William Shakespeare* (*BNW*, 110).[2] Much of the parodic resonance of Huxley's satire of the advancement of science as it effects human individualism relies on the relationship thus established between the possibilities of human freedom and transformation available in the tragic landscapes and the high Romantic greenworlds of Shakespearian drama, on the one hand, and the grey and crushing demand for conformity and social stability in AF 632, on the other. The innocence and naive expectation of Shakespeare's Miranda is parodically echoed by Savage (who himself uses the phrase 'brave new world' on no fewer than three occasions), who will eventually be driven to tragedy by the incompatibility of his own emotions with the strictures of the new, conformist civilization into which he is introduced.

The internalized parody of Gray's 'Elegy' that opens the fifth chapter of Huxley's novel is quite explicit in its references to its source or target text. In the chapter, Henry Foster and one of the secondary characters in the novel, Lenina Crown, have been compelled to abandon their game of golf as twilight closes in on the course. Huxley writes:

> By eight o'clock the light was failing. The loud speakers in the tower of the Stoke Poges Club House began, in a more than human tenor, to announce the closing of the courses. Lenina and Henry abandoned their game and walked back towards the Club. From the grounds of the Internal and External Secretion Trust came the lowing of those thousands of cattle which provided, with their

hormones and their milk, the raw materials for the great factory at Farnham Royal.

An incessant buzzing of helicopters filled the twilight. Every two and a half minutes a bell and the screech of whistles announced the departure of one of the light monorail trains which carried the lower-caste golfers back from their separate course to the metropolis.

(BNW, 66)

The reference to Stoke Poges in Buckinghamshire—eventually the churchyard site of Thomas Gray's own tomb and thought by many to have been the precise landscape that inspired his famous 'Elegy'—deliberately draws the reader to the unavoidable echoes of Gray's original in the passage. The opening stanzas of Gray's poem, of course, had described the solitary poet in the evening landscape:

The curfew tolls the knell of parting day,
The lowing herd wind slowly o'er the lea,
The plowman homeward plods his weary way,
And leaves the world to darkness and to me.

Now fades the glimmering landscape on the sight,
And all the air a solemn stillness holds,
Save where the beetle wheels his droning flight,
And drowsy tinklings lull the distant folds:

Save that from yonder ivy-mantled tow'r,
The moping owl does to the moon complain
Of such as, wand'ring near her secret bow'r,
Molest her ancient solitary reign.[3]

In Huxley's brave new world, however, the 'curfew' is tolled not by the bell in the local churchyard, but by the 'loudspeakers' in the Club House Tower; the few lowing herds of Gray's original have been replaced by the lowing of 'thousands of cattle' being mass farmed for their hormones and milk; the lone plowman of the 'Elegy' returning home from the fields has been replicated

by the vast multitude of 'lower-caste' golfers who are being fer-
ried by monorail back to London. The other, companionable
sensations of Gray's rural twilight—the 'glimmering' landscape,
the 'droning' beetle, the 'drowsy' tinklings, the 'moping' owl—
have similarly been overwhelmed by the cacophony of noises
generated by the new world order—the 'buzzing' of many
helicopters, and the incessant bells and 'screeching' whistles of
innumerable trains.

The exact purpose of Huxley's parody—its function within
the larger parodic stance of the novel as a whole—seems at
first slightly ambiguous. Huxley would appear to be suggesting
that his own brave new world of the future is one in which
the 'Elegy's' meditation on the equality achieved by all human
beings in death has been superseded entirely by the society's
deliberate and calculated inequalities in intelligence and ability.
Gray's original had puzzled over the fact that the very same
churchyard might well contain the remains of some potential
Cromwell 'guiltless of his country's blood', just as it might at
the same time hold the body of some 'mute, inglorious Milton'.
The poet of the 'Elegy' is somewhat at a loss to explain the
social and political conditions that dictate just who will achieve
fame or infamy (or who will even attain literacy) in the public
sphere. Individual destinies are affected and in many cases
determined by circumstances far beyond human control. In
Huxley's parody, however, the potentials once determined only
by the hand of an inscrutable God or Fate have become the
provenance of man himself; there is little or no chance that any
'Cromwell' created by Huxley's society would ever conceivably
be allowed to develop into anything other than precisely the
military machine its creators intended it to be. Likewise, one
need no longer stand in need of the fatal heroics of any John
Hampdens; all men are paradoxically equal because they have
been created with a calculated degree of inequality.

Yet Huxley's parody—here specifically but in the novel as a
whole, as well—quite vividly suggests that anything that once
made the world an admittedly unpredictable yet livable place
has been completely obliterated. Possessing no individual char-
acteristics, humans have lost their own capacity to appreciate

the very inconveniences and unpredictability that once made life worth living. As John Savage contends passionately with Mustapha Mond—Resident Controller for Western Europe and one of ten such officials in the world—when he rejects the world of the novel in a climactic scene towards the end of Huxley's narrative:

> 'I don't want comfort. I want God, I want poetry, I want real danger, I want freedom, I want goodness. I want sin.'
>
> 'In fact,' said Mustapha Mond, 'you're claiming the right to be unhappy.'
>
> 'All right then,' said the Savage defiantly, 'I'm claiming the right to be unhappy.'
>
> 'Not to mention the right to grow old and ugly and impotent; the right to have syphilis and cancer; the right to have too little to eat; the right to be lousy; the right to live in constant apprehension of what might happen tomorrow; the right to catch typhoid; the right to be tortured by unspeakable pains of every kind.'
>
> There was a long silence.
>
> 'I claim them all,' said the Savage at last.
>
> (*BNW*, 192)

Oppressed by the artificial happiness created by Huxley's society, Savage thus claims as his birthright the entire range of human experience—both good and bad—just as his constant recourse to Shakespearian language reflects the inherent human capacity for both tragic and comic or 'romantic' behaviour. Savage alone among the characters in the novel would have understood the significance of a poem such as the 'Elegy'—a poem that emphasizes the accidental transience of life, and the solace to be found even in the levelling soil of the churchyard. . . .

Before his final visit to yet another factory, where he witnesses a 'long caterpillar of men and women' (*BNW*, 134) lined up to receive their daily ration of the sedative 'soma', Savage is taken by 'taxiporter' to Eton College. Huxley describes his arrival at the once prestigious school:

At Eton they alighted on the roof of the Upper School. On the opposite side of School Yard, the fifty-two stories of Lupton's Tower gleamed white in the sunshine. College on their left and, on their right, the School Community Singery reared their venerable piles of ferro-concrete and vita-glass. In the centre of the quadrangle stood the quaint old chrome-steel statue of Our Ford.

(*BNW*, 131–2)

The passage quite clearly evokes the beginning of the opening stanzas of Gray's 'Ode on a Distant Prospect of Eton College':

Ye distant spires, ye antique towers,
That crown the watr'y glade,
Where grateful science still adores
Her Henry's holy shade.

(Gray, 'Eton Ode', lines 1–4)

The 'distant spires' and 'antique towers' of Eton's historical past have undergone a radical transformation. Lupton's Tower—an actual sixteenth-century building on the East side of Eton's School Yard and named after Robert Lupton, Provost of Eton from 1504 to 1535—has obviously been demolished and replaced by a gleaming white, fifty-two storey tower block; the Chapel has similarly been replaced by the glass and concrete 'Community Singery'. The 'holy shade' of King Henry VI, who founded Eton in 1440 and whose venerable statue stands in the centre of School Yard, has made way for an already 'quaint' and parodic antique statue of Henry Ford.

Although said still to be reserved for the education of 'exclusively upper-caste' (*BNW*, 132) boys and girls, Eton has effectively been reduced to yet another scientifically oriented indoctrination centre. If chapter five's parody of the 'Elegy' had to some extent lamented the loss of individuality and of individual potential in Huxley's world, the 'Eton Ode' parody of chapter eleven furthers that same lament. Confessing himself to be 'a trifle bewildered' by the College curriculum, Savage questions the school's head mistress:

'Do they read Shakespeare?' asked the Savage as they walked on their way to the Biochemical Laboratories, past the School Library.

'Certainly not,' said the Head Mistress, blushing.

'Our library', said Dr. Gaffney, 'contains only books of reference. If our young people need distraction, they can get it at the feelies. We don't encourage them to engage in any solitary amusements.'

(*BNW*, 133)

The reference to the discouragement of 'solitary amusements' would immediately have recalled to many of Huxley's readers the cautious celebration of precisely such self-sought isolation from the crowd in the fourth stanza of Gray's ode:

Some bold adventurers disdain
The limits of their little reign,
 And unknown regions dare descry:
Still as they run they look behind,
They hear a voice in every wind,
 And snatch a fearful joy.

(Gray, 'Eton Ode', lines 35–40)

The nervous tension of transgression—the 'fearful joy' of trespass—is a sensation that is unlikely ever to be experienced even by the Alpha-Double-First inmates of tomorrow's Eton.

Huxley's conclusion of Savage's visit to the school amounts to an outright, parodic refutation of the 'Eton Ode's' now aphoristic closing lines: 'where Ignorance is bliss, / 'Tis folly to be wise' (lines 99–100). Gray himself had arrived at such a conclusion (which must be taken in context) only after a careful consideration as an adult of the psychic benefits of a childhood innocent of any knowledge of the generally dismal experience of life itself (his crucial, qualifying 'where'—in the sense of 'wherein' or 'in such circumstances' is too often excised or replaced by those quoting his lines). I have argued elsewhere that although Gray emphasizes the kinds of knowledge that any mature individual would gratefully avoid (such as Anger,

Care, Sorrow, and the painful proximity of Death itself), and although he presents by means of vivid personification in the second half of the poem the manner in which the poignant idealism of youth is gradually unmasked as illusions by the advance of maturity, he nevertheless ends his poem with an attempt to shield the young from such dread knowledge:[4]

> Yet, ah! Why should they know their fate,
> Since sorrow never comes too late,
> And happiness too swiftly flies?
> Thought would destroy their paradise . . .
>
> (Gray, 'Eton Ode', lines 95–8)

Huxley's parodic redaction of Gray's lines represents a complete and explicit refutation of Gray's protective impulse in the new world of Huxley's future. . . .

The respective parodies of the 'Elegy' and the 'Eton Ode' in chapters five and eleven—poems that had emphasized mortal cost and the reality of human pain and suffering in a more natural social environment—are perfectly encapsulated within the novel's larger more comprehensive reference to the world of Shakespearian tragedy and romance.

Notes

2. Aldous Huxley, *Brave New World* (London: Grafton, 1977 [1932]); all references to Huxley's novel are to this edition.

3. Thomas Gray, 'Elegy Written in a Country Churchyard' (lines 1–12) in *Selected Poems*, ed. Robert Mack (London: J. M. Dent, 1996). All references to Gray's poetry are to this edition.

4. See Robert L. Mack, *Thomas Gray: A Life* (London: Yale University Press, 2000), 324–9.

CASS R. SUNSTEIN ON HUXLEY AND GEORGE ORWELL'S CONTRASTING VIEWS OF LOVE AND SEX

While there are a number of portrayals of sex in *Nineteen Eighty-Four*, there are only two love stories, involving two couples: Julia and Winston is one, and Winston and O'Brien the other; the most erotically charged, even intense scenes involve the latter. In a way the whole book is structured around a love triangle, in which O'Brien extinguishes the erotic connection between Julia and Winston, marking the triumph of the Party against a "blow" that had threatened it, and reestablishing both chastity and political orthodoxy. . . .

We might compare in this regard the very different presentation of the relation between sexual freedom and political freedom in Huxley's *Brave New World*. There sexual promiscuity is a kind of opiate of the masses, consistently encouraged partly in order to discourage political rebellion. Both novels portray the death of the individual soul, but with major differences: Where *Nineteen Eighty-Four* is a nightmare vision of Communism or Fascism, *Brave New World* is a nightmare vision of triumphant capitalism. We might even identify a Huxley hypothesis, one that appears to compete directly with Orwell's: Sexual activity diverts people from engaging in political causes, and it ought therefore to be encouraged by a government that seeks a quiescent population. On this view, sexual promiscuity is depoliticizing, soul-destroying, a twin to soma, antagonistic to rebellion. Some political movements have in fact accepted this view, and it is easy to see how it might be true. We can imagine the possibilities described in the accompanying matrix.

	Sexual repression	Sexual freedom
Political repression	Orwell's *Nineteen Eighty-Four*	Huxley's *Brave New World*
Political freedom	Many dissident groups	One understanding of contemporary America

On this view, Huxley's hypothesis is the antonym to Orwell's. But along one dimension, it is only apparently competing. The key point is that Huxley, like Orwell, identifies sexual activity with political passivity. In Orwell, the state seeks marching, even a form of fanaticism; in Huxley, the state seeks a kind of pleased, vacant indifference. Sexual repression is, in *Nineteen Eighty-Four*, a necessary way of "bottling down some powerful instinct and using it as a driving force" (111); in *Brave New World*, the society is infantilized and pacified through catering to that same instinct. Thus it is that in Orwell's world, a form of sex that is not a "frigid little ceremony" (110) is a threat to the political order, whereas in Huxley's, the threat comes from a refusal of sex, or of soma, which will be and will produce rebellion. Compare Winston to Julia, who appears to have little interest in politics, and who says, "I'm not interested in the next generation, dear." When Winston says, "You're only a rebel from the waist downwards," she does not object but instead finds the statement "brilliantly witty" (129).

But there are other possibilities, very different from Orwell's and Huxley's shared view. It may be that sexual love can actually fuel political activity, by expanding the imagination and promoting empathic engagement with the lives of others. Probably we need to distinguish here, as Orwell does not, among different kinds of sexuality. It is not as if there is a choice only between "the Party's sexual puritanism" and "sexual privation" (Orwell's phrases) on the one hand and "making love" on the other. Promiscuous relationships are not all the same; nor are enduring, passionate relationships. Promiscuous relationships may have different effects from enduring, passionate relationships. The connection between any one of these and political activity depends on many independent variables.

All this may not be quite fair to Orwell. He also seems to have another point in mind. It has to do with how sexuality is connected with individuality and self-expression, with the rejection of conformity, with what he seems to see as the truest and most distinctive self, anarchic and not governable. It is this that presents the deepest danger to the Party. Orwell is not speaking here of love or of intimate relations with individual persons: "Not merely the love of one person, but the animal instinct, the simple undifferentiated desire: that was the force that would tear the Party to pieces" (105). Here, too, there is an interesting relationship with Huxley, who portrays promiscuity as soulless, as an erasure of individuality, as a form of conformity.

Both Huxley and Orwell may have a particular conception of authentic sexuality in view, and they may not be so different. The contrast is that Orwell portrays "the animal instinct, the simple undifferentiated desire" as active and a threat to political orthodoxy, something that, once unleashed, will lead to rebellion. O'Brien appears to agree. Winston's torture and castration produce a kind of docility, even serenity, that paves the way for, or that is, acceptance of Big Brother and death.

Orwell's conception of sexuality as an "animal instinct," and as an expression of something ungovernable and personal, may be right; certainly there is truth in it. But sexuality can itself be a product of social practices; it should not be naturalized, and opposed, as "true self," to cultural constraint. We do not know the extent to which sexual drives are themselves a product of private and public authority. Orwell tends to naturalize the "sex instinct" (as the very term suggests). This is an under-explored point in the novel itself, where sexual drives seem to be something beyond the reach of politics or the Party, except through after-the-fact techniques of the kind used by O'Brien. Perhaps this is not Orwell's full position; Winston's early fantasies of sexual violence might be taken as a product of the particular social circumstances of Party domination. But this point is not much elaborated, nor is it brought into contact with Julia's claims about the nature and consequence of sexual activity. . . .

Orwell suggests that totalitarian governments favor "sexual puritanism," which induces "hysteria," something that such governments mobilize in their own favor. This is the image of patriotic frenzy as "sex gone sour." On this view, sexual freedom embodies freedom and individualism, and it is the deepest enemy of a totalitarian state. A state that allows sexual freedom will be unable to repress its citizens. This is why O'Brien must achieve victory over Julia.

But it is possible to imagine other, equally plausible views. "Sexual privation" might indeed induce hysteria, but of the sort that leads to rebellion and thus serves as an obstacle to a successful totalitarian government. I have suggested that in the face of existing social norms, many people who are sexually active are also likely to be political rebels, because of something in their character (itself perhaps a product of early childhood or genetic predispositions). And sexual freedom, even promiscuity, might be encouraged by totalitarian governments, in order to divert the citizenry and to induce apathy. (This is Huxley's thesis.) Or we might reject the idea that the only two options are "privation" and "freedom" (as understood by both Orwell and Huxley). The real question might be what sorts of intimate relationships people are allowed to make with one another.

RICHARD A. POSNER ON THE NOVEL'S DISTORTION OF CONTEMPORARY SOCIETY

Huxley's novel is much more high-tech than Orwell's. This is not surprising; Huxley came from a distinguished scientific family and studied to be a doctor, whereas Orwell had no familial or educational background in science. Futuristic technology is a pervasive feature of the society depicted in *Brave New World* and is meticulously described and explained. It is of three types. The first is reproductive technology. Contraception has been made foolproof yet does not interfere with sexual pleasure. So sex has been separated reliably from procreation at last and, at the same time, procreation has been separated from sex. Ova extracted from ovaries are mixed in the laboratory with sperm, and the fertilized ova are brought to term in incubators. The procedure has enabled the perfection of eugenic breeding, yielding five genetically differentiated castes, ranging from high-IQ Alphas to moronic Epsilons, to enable a perfect matching of genetic endowment with society's task needs.[15]

Second is mind- and body-altering technology, including hypnopaedia (hypnosis during sleep), Pavlovian conditioning, elaborate cosmetic surgery, and happiness pills (*soma*, similar to our Prozac, but nonprescription and taken continually by everyone). For the elderly, there are "gonadal hormones" and "transfusion of young blood."[16] Third is happiness-inducing entertainment technology, including television, synthetic music, movies that gratify the five senses (the "Feelies"), and, for the Alphas, personal helicopters for vacations.

These technological advances are represented as having profound effects. They induce mindless contentment, including guiltless promiscuous sex. They induce complete intellectual and cultural vacuity, and complete political passivity. Marriage, the family, and parenthood—all conceived of as sources of misery, tension, and painful strong emotions—have gone by the board. But none of these consequences is presented as an *unintended* consequence of technological innovation, which is our fear of technology and a fear that the economics of technology suggests some rational basis for. Technology in *Brave New World* is the slave of a utilitarian ideology. Above everything else, Huxley's novel is a send-up of utilitarianism. "The higher castes . . . [must not] lose their faith in happiness as the Sovereign Good and take to believing, instead, that the goal was somewhere beyond, somewhere outside the present human sphere; that the purpose of life was not the maintenance of well-being, but some intensification and refining of consciousness, some enlargement of knowledge."[17] Technology has enabled the creation of the utilitarian paradise, in which happiness is maximized, albeit at the cost of everything that makes human beings interesting.[18] The Savage is unhappy but vital; the "civilized" people are fatuous, empty. The role of technology is to create the conditions in which a tiny elite can combine complete control over social, political, and economic life with the achievement of material abundance. This is an echo of the 1930s belief in the efficacy of central planning.

The topicality of satire, well illustrated in Huxley's novel by the caste system that is obviously a satiric commentary on the English class system and by the exhibiting of the Savage and his mother to the shocked Londoners as exotic specimens of New World savagery (though the two of them are in fact English), invites us to consider conditions in England when *Brave New World* was written. It was in the depths of a world depression that Keynes was teaching had resulted from insufficient consumer demand and could be cured only by aggressive government intervention. Capitalism was believed to have failed, for lack of sufficient coordination or rationalization, resulting in excessive, destructive competition. Capitalism (competition, the "free market") was not merely unjust; it was inefficient. There was also great anxiety about falling birth rates and the quality of the genetic pool.

All these concerns are mirrored in *Brave New World*. One of the salient features of the society depicted in it is consumerism, which encompasses planned obsolescence and a "throwaway" mentality ("ending is better than mending").[19] People are brainwashed to want ever more, ever newer consumer goods, lest consumer demand flag. This is an example of how everything is planned and directed, down to the smallest detail of culture, technology, and consumption, from the center. And eugenic breeding solves the population and gene-pool problems. The society of *Brave New World* is the "logical" outcome of reform measures advocated by advanced thinkers in England and other countries during the depression. Developing the logic of an existing social system to an absurd or repulsive extreme (Huxley appears to have thought it the latter, not doubting its feasibility) is a typical technique of satire; we shall see it at work in *Nineteen Eighty-Four* as well.

Without technology, the "solution" that Huxley limns to 1930s-type problems would not be workable. But the technology plays a supporting rather than initiating role. It is the tool of a philosophical and economic vision. There is no sense that technology has merely evolved, unplanned, to a level that makes the regimented, trivial society depicted in the novel likely, let alone inevitable. There is no law of unintended consequences operating. Technology enables but does not dictate.

What makes *Brave New World* still a good "read" today is mainly the fact that so many of its predictions of futuristic technology and morality have come or are rapidly coming to pass. Sex has been made largely safe for pleasure by the invention of methods of contraception that at once are reliable and do not interfere with the pleasure of sex, while, as I noted earlier, a variety of other technological advances, ranging from better care of pregnant women and of infants to household labor-saving devices and advances in the medical treatment of infertility and the automation of the workplace, have (along with the contraceptive advances, and safe abortion on demand) freed women from the traditional restrictions on their sexual freedom.[20] The result is a climate of sexual freedom, and of public obsession with sex and sexual pleasure, much like that depicted in Huxley's novel, though "mother" is not yet a dirty word as it literally is in the novel and marriage has not yet been abolished, though the marriage rate has fallen considerably.

The society of happy thoughtless philistines depicted by Huxley will thus strike some readers as an exaggeration rather than a distortion of today's America. We, too, are awash in happiness pills, of both the legal and illegal variety, augmented by increasingly ambitious cosmetic surgery to make us happier about our appearance. We are enveloped by entertainment technology to a degree that even Huxley could not imagine; in our society too "cleanliness is next to fordliness."[21] We have a horror of physical aging and even cultivate infantilism—adults dressing and talking like children. "Alphas are so conditioned that they do not *have* to be infantile in their emotional behaviour. But that is all the more reason for their making a special effort to conform. It is their duty to be infantile, even against their inclination."[22] We live in the present; our slogan, too, might be, "Never put off till tomorrow the fun you can have today."[23] Popular culture has everywhere triumphed over high culture; the past has been largely forgotten. We consider it our duty as well as our right to pursue happiness right to the edge of the grave. In the "Park Lane Hospital for the Dying . . . we try to create a thoroughly pleasant atmosphere . . . , something between a first-class hotel and a feely-palace."[24] Our culture is saturated with sex. Shopping is the national pastime. Although Americans are not entirely passive politically, we are largely content with the status quo, we are largely free from envy and resentment, the major political parties are copies of each other, and a 1930s style depression seems unimaginable to most of us. Depression in both its senses is becoming unimaginable.

We may even be moving, albeit slowly, toward a greater genetic differentiation of classes, although not by the mechanism depicted in *Brave New World*—yet that mechanism will soon be feasible. With the decline of arranged marriage and the breaking down of taboos against interracial, interethnic, and religiously mixed marriage, prospective marriage partners can be expected to be sorted more by "real" similarities, including intelligence.[25] IQ has a significant heritable component, so the implication of more perfect assortative mating is that the IQ distribution will widen in future generations.

But all this has come (or is coming) about without foresight or direction, contrary to the implication of Huxley's novel. It turns out that a society can attain "Fordism"[26]—the rationalization, the systematization, of production that was originally symbolized by the assembly line—without centralization. Huxley was mistaken to equate efficiency with collectivization.[27] Our society has no utilitarian master plan and no utilitarian master planner. Nothing corresponds to *Brave New World*'s "Controllers," the successors to Dostoyevsky's Grand Inquisitor: "Happiness is a hard master—particularly other people's happiness."[28] And despite its resemblance to Huxley's dystopia, what we have seems to most people, even the thinking people, rather closer to Utopia.

Notes

15. "We decant our babies as socialized human beings, as Alphas or Epsilons, as sewage workers or future . . . Directors of Hatcheries," *Brave New World*, p. 13.

16. Ibid., 54.

17. Ibid., 177.

18. "'Yes, everybody's happy now,' echoed Lenina. They had heard the words repeated a hundred and fifty times every night for twelve years" (when they were children). Ibid., p. 75.

19. Ibid., 49.

20. "In some areas, despite its being a dystopia, *Brave New World* offers women a better deal than the contemporary British society of the 1930s. There is no housework, no wifely subjugation, no need to balance children and a career." June Deery, "Technology and Gender in Aldous Huxley's Alternative (?) Worlds," in *Critical Essays on Aldous Huxley*, ed. Jerome Meckier (New York: G. K. Hall, 1996), pp. 103, 105.

21. Huxley, *Brave New World*, 110.

22. Ibid., 98.

23. Ibid., 93.

24. Ibid., 198–99.

25. On the tendency to "assortative" mating—likes mating with likes—see Gary S. Becker, *A Treatise on the Family*, enlarged ed. (Cambridge: Harvard University Press, 1991), ch. 4.

26. Henry Ford is the Karl Marx of the society depicted in *Brave New World*. Instead of making the sign of the cross, the denizens of the world make a T, which stands of course for Ford's Model T.

27. His equation of them is well discussed in James Sexton, "Brave New World and the Rationalization of Industry," *Critical Essays on Aldous Huxley*, p. 88.

28. Huxley, *Brave New World*, 227.

CAREY SNYDER ON HUXLEY'S AND D.H. LAWRENCE'S USE OF THE PAST

[D.H.] Lawrence and [Aldous] Huxley were engaged in a parallel project of satirizing what I will call "ethnological tourism": tourism that takes travelers to sites such as the tropics, reservations, and ethnological exhibits, mimicking modern ethnology's goal of observing traditional customs and ceremonies firsthand.[7] In satirizing the way that tourism transforms the reservations and pueblos of the Southwest into ethnological spectacle, Lawrence and Huxley go beyond the modern trope of anti-tourism;[8] they explore the potentially destructive effects of cultural spectatorship on indigenous cultures, and thus implicitly critique the modes of observation and representation that characterize modern ethnography as well. Coming at the vogue of the Indian from two very different perspectives— Lawrence as a primitivist longing to reconnect with lost origins, Huxley as a satirist wishing to expose primitivism as a utopian fantasy—these writers nonetheless provide a similar critique of the way both tourism and ethnography potentially disrupt local traditions, objectifying indigenous people and commodifying their culture. . . .

Huxley had little patience with contemporaries who sought alternatives to civilized life in what he regarded as fanciful perceptions of primitive societies. In a 1931 essay, he pokes fun at ethnological tourists, remarking that of late "the few remaining primitive peoples of the earth have achieved a prodigious popularity among those with wishes to fulfill" (*Music* 129). Implicating Lawrence's writings in particular, Huxley proclaims that "the past has become a compensatory Utopia. . . . With every advance of industrial civilization the savage past will be more and more appreciated, and the cult of D. H. Lawrence's *Dark God* may be expected to spread through an ever-widening circle of worshippers" (*Music* 128, 131). In contrast to Lawrence, Huxley envisioned primitive societies in largely Hobbesian terms, and declared unambiguously that it was futile to try to go back to what both writers imagined was a prior evolutionary stage. The two writers come at the vogue of the Indian, then, from very different angles: Lawrence, seeking to penetrate the touristy façade to connect with ancient traditions, and Huxley, rejecting the idea of establishing such a connection as mere Romantic idealism.

While debunking the construction of the Southwest as a primitive utopia, *Brave New World* simultaneously debunks a competing model of ideal society endorsed by World's Fairs, which seemed to provide "a map to future perfection" in the shape of a world made safer, easier, more efficient, and more enjoyable by technology and science (Rydell 219). Conjoining these two visions was not unique: at the 1915 Panama-California Expo, organizers situated a model farm, complete with modern farm equipment, a fruit-bearing orchard, and electricity, alongside the Painted Desert exhibit displaying Southwest Indians. The juxtaposition was intended, in the words of one of the fair organizers, to provide "a sermon" on progress: to reinforce the impression of Native Americans as "the vanished although romantic past and Anglo-America as the triumphant future" (Kropp, *Great Southwest* 38). The structure of Huxley's *Brave New World* reproduces the logic of the Panama-California Expo by juxtaposing the Savage Reservation and the Fordian new world. Rather than an idealized, pastoral representation of "vanishing America," however, the Savage Reservation is defined by its harshness, dirt, and supposedly barbaric customs; a vacation there superficially reinforces the desirability of the new world with its hygiene, efficiency, and emphasis on pleasure. If, as with the Panama-Pacific, the ideological message is that Indians are quaint but that progress and conquest are inevitable and good, the shallow character Lenina gets the message: "progress *is* lovely, isn't it?" (77). Huxley ironizes this response, subverting the rosy narrative of progress and cheery futurism of the World's Fairs, by making the hygienic, efficient, hyper-technological new world a nightmare society.

When John the Savage visits Eton on his tour of the New World, he learns that the reservation where he was raised is regarded as "a place which, owing to unfavourable climatic or geological conditions, or poverty of natural resources, has not been worth the expense of civilizing" (124). Given the harsh conditions of the environment and the "civilized" characters' derogatory view of the natives' way of life (the warden tells Lenina and Bernard that the Indians are "absolute savages" who "still preserve their repulsive habits and customs" [79]), the idea of taking a holiday on a New Mexican "Savage Reservation" is made to seem ludicrous in *Brave New World*. By representing the reservation as a popular tourist destination, Huxley mocks the contemporary craze for travel to the Southwest: Lenina eagerly accepts Bernard's invitation to New Mexico, explaining that she "always wanted to see a savage reservation," and the Director of Hatcheries and Conditioning tells Bernard, "I had the same idea as you. . . . Wanted to have a look at the savages. Got a permit for New Mexico and went there for my summer holiday" (33, 96).

Surrounded by a straight fence that is said to represent "the geometrical symbol of triumphant human purpose," the reservation is constructed as a prison or zoo (80). That the "triumphant purpose" of the fence is forcible containment is made clear by the pilot's sinister pronouncement, "There is no escape from a Savage Reservation," a warning he means to mute by adding that the savages are "perfectly tame. . . . They've got enough experience of gas bombs to know that they mustn't play any tricks" (78, 81). The fence serves not only to contain its inhabitants, but also to frame them: following Lawrence, Huxley highlights the exploitative dynamics of confining indigenous people to reservations and then exposing them to the inquisitive gaze of the dominant society. As in the Joy Zone of the World's Fair or in Harvey's Southwest, on Huxley's Savage

Reservation, native life is viewed as entertainment: "Everything they do is funny," the pilot remarks pointing at "a sullen young savage" whose oppressed demeanor belies this statement (81). Huxley's characters regard the quotidian life of the "savages" as a tableau for their observation: sighting an "almost naked Indian" climbing down a ladder, Lenina grips Bernard's arm and urges him, "Look" (84)—the single word highlighting the principle activity of the ethnological tourist. Whereas the tourists in Lawrence's essays thrill to exotic otherness, Huxley's character recoils in disgust, repulsed by the man's wrinkled face and toothless mouth, an anti-image of new world youthfulness.

Yet if both writers satirize tourists who regard native life as spectacle, Huxley does not share Lawrence's faith that behind the tourist façade lurks a genuine culture worth reclaiming. For Lawrence, fencing in indigenous cultures is a metaphor for civilization's unfortunate repression of its instinctual side: "'Till now, in sheer terror of ourselves, we have turned our backs on the jungle, fenced it in with an enormous entanglement of barbed wire and declared it did not exist . . . Yet unless we proceed to connect ourselves up with our own primeval sources, we shall degenerate" ("The Novel and Feelings" 757). In theory, if not in practice, Lawrence believed that tearing down the fence to connect with indigenous cultures was the last hope for a decadent civilization. In *Beyond the Mexique Bay*, Huxley explicitly rejects Lawrence's primitivism: "When man became an intellectual and spiritual being, he paid for his new privileges with a treasure of intuitions, of emotional spontaneity, of sensuality still innocent of all self-consciousness. Lawrence [mistakenly] thought that we should abandon the new privileges in return for the old treasure" (261). In essays such as "Indians and an Englishman," Lawrence hardly seems like one ready to abandon the privileges of his subject position as an Englishman; his fantasy of connection with Indians is wholly reliant on an implied distance between Indians and Englishmen that he carefully enforces. Still, for Lawrence, a rapprochement between "civilized" and "primitive" life is at least desirable, whereas for Huxley, giving up (or fencing in) "primeval sources" is the price of civilization. . . .

In *Brave New World*, Huxley finds an opportunity to write his mock ethnography of modern society, with a particular focus on modern sex lives. The Controller Mustapha Mond contrasts the "appalling dangers of [old fashioned] family life," encompassing misery, sadism, and chastity, with the relative ease of the social structures and sexual practices of the new world. In defending new world sexuality, he cites as model societies both "the savages of Samoa," whose children played "promiscuously among the hibiscus blossoms," and the Trobriand Islanders, among whom fatherhood was supposedly unknown (28). The analogy between Samoan and Trobriand "savages" and the characters of the new world is reinforced by the description of "civilized" children, "naked in the warm June sunshine," sexually frolicking next to blooming shrubs and murmuring bees, and, a few pages later, "naked children furtive in the undergrowth" (21, 31). These passages echo Mead's description of "lusty" Samoans engaged in casual romantic "trysts" among palm fronds and hibiscus blossoms, in the opening pages of *Coming of Age in Samoa* (12–13). The tie between the "savages" studied by Mead and Malinowski and the people of the new world is also reinforced by references to climate: in the new world, embryos are "hatched" in a "tropical" environment, and soma offers an escape to what sounds like the "tropical paradise" of modern ads: "the warm, the richly coloured, the infinitely friendly world of a *soma*-holiday" (7, 60). In *Brave New World*, England has gone tropical and, paradoxically, given the reign of technology and science in the new world, England has gone native.

While the playful analogy turns the English into ethnographic others, enacting Huxley's fantasy of writing a mock ethnography of curious English customs, the point is not finally that all cultures are relative, or that we are "one family of man" with negligible differences among us. Instead, conceived in an increasingly outmoded evolutionary framework, the formulation is meant to broadcast an attitude of irony concerning the new world's dismissal of traditional family values, the abrogation of monogamy and of fatherhood marking the pathetic descent of the citizens of the new world into primitive irresponsibility. Gesturing to the children of the new world naked in the undergrowth and concluding his discourse on the cultures of Samoa and the Trobriand Islands, the Controller declares triumphantly, "Extremes . . . meet. For the good reason that they were made to meet" (28). Huxley adopts this idea of wedding the two worlds of primitive and civilized societies from Lawrence—for whom such a union is a fantasy, while for Huxley, it is a misguided quest.

Notes

7. Some explanation is required for my use of "ethnological tourism" rather than "cultural" or "ethnic tourism," both commonly employed in tourism studies. "Cultural tourism" construes culture in a broad sense, embracing travel to the Lake District to buy Beatrix Potter paraphernalia as well as travel to Waikiki to watch staged performances of fire ceremonies. (For elaboration of these terms, see Chris Rojek and John Urry.) I use "ethnological" rather than "cultural" to refer more narrowly to tourism that seeks so-called premodern or traditional cultures as its main object, following in the footsteps of modern ethnologists such as Ruth Bunzel and Margaret Mead. "Ethnic tourism"—defined by Van den Berghe and Keyes as that where "the prime attraction is the cultural exoticism of the local population and its artifacts (clothing, architecture, theater, music, dance, plastic arts)"—is closer to the meaning I intend (345). I employ "ethnological" rather than "ethnic," however, to emphasize the potential bond between the ethnologist and the tourist, figures who often work in the same settings and share some of the same objectives, most notably aiming to see "natives as they really live." A final note: Though the terms "ethnology," "ethnography," and "anthropology" acquire different connotations later in the twentieth century, I use "ethnology" to refer to studies of cultures conducted in the field, as opposed to armchair theorizing. This usage is consistent with professional nomenclature of the day, as in the US American *Ethnology* Bureau, and with Lawrence's and Huxley's respective usages of the term.

8. See Dean MacCannell and James Buzard.

JOHN COUGHLIN ON *BRAVE NEW WORLD* AND RALPH ELLISON'S *INVISIBLE MAN*

Just recently having completed in their entirety both [Ralph Ellison's] *Invisible Man* and [Huxley's] *Brave New World*, I am once again struck by how similar they are in theme. Both books are, without a doubt, political in nature, and at this level, seem completely dissimilar—*Invisible Man* attempts to illuminate the social entrapment of black Americans, while *Brave New World* cautions against an over reliance on technology and the amorality it can potentially inspire. At a deeper level, however, both books are also about the status of the individual in society, and it is here that there is a remarkable similarity between the two novels. For in both, we see men fighting against societies that devalue their individuality and thereby lessen their sense of identity and self-worth. "I've always tried to create characters who were pretty forthright in stating what they felt society should be," said Ellison in a 1963 interview (Geller 85). This statement captures the underlying theme of both novels: that an ideal society is one that is founded upon the ability of individuals to assert themselves freely and without prejudice. Close examination of both works show that while they are wildly different in many ways, at this one level, they are very much the same. . . .

"All novels are about certain minorities," says Ellison, "The individual is a minority. The universal in the novel—and isn't that what we're all clamoring for these days?—is reached only through the description of the specific man in a specific circumstance" (Chester 9). Huxley says something along the same lines in the forward to a later edition of *Brave New World*: "The theme of *Brave New World* is not the advancement of science as such; it is the advancement of science as it affects human individuals" (Huxley 16). Both statements suggest that Ellison and Huxley are more concerned about the state of the individual than the state of society, and this is an important distinction for one of the more subtle points of both novels is that the health of society is determined by the health of the individuals of which it is composed.

The sickness inherent in both societies becomes apparent early on. In *Invisible Man*, Ellison depicts a classed society in which a select group of people uses the narrator for their own selfish purposes, refusing to see the inherent individual worth beyond the color of his skin. One of our first examples of this is when Mr. Norton, the wealthy supporter of the institute the narrator attends, describes how the students there are all building blocks in his destiny. . . ."'That has been my real life's work, not my banking or my researches, but my first hand organizing of human life'" (42). By asserting that he is responsible for "organizing" the young narrator's life, Mr. Norton is implying that he is somehow responsible for the man's future worth to society. . . . In order for the narrator of *Invisible Man* to achieve humanity, therefore, he must shed the misconception that his life has been organized by anyone but himself and count any achievement as solely his own.

Mr. Norton's use of the word "organization" is not without significance when comparing *Invisible Man* to *Brave New World*, for in this second novel, we see a society where organization has been taken to the extreme. In the Brave New World, the highest tiers of individuals (labeled as Alphas and Betas and led by the illustrious Mustapha Mond, an Alpha double plus) have organized the more numerous lower classes (Deltas and Epsilons) into what they consider efficient and contented sub-races, "modeled" on nothing so cold and inhuman as an iceberg: "The optimum population," said Mustapha Mond, "is modeled on the iceberg—eight ninths below the water, one ninth above" (172). The Alphas and Betas believe that they have invented the perfect workforce—one that is happy, well organized, and, above all, incapable of asserting individual will against the upper classes because of lower intellectual capabilities and preoccupation with work. . . .

The idea of keeping an individual preoccupied with meaningless tasks so that he might never question his own individuality is an important one, for throughout *Invisible Man* we are reminded of the line "keep the nigger running." . . .

The citizens of *Brave New World* are constantly running, too. From birth they are conditioned via "hypnopaedia" to dread being alone, for isolation breeds introspection that in turns fosters a sense of individuality. This is expressed in a wonderfully satiric scene where Bernard takes Lenina out on their first date—he suggests that they go for a walk along the mall and talk, but she, finding such an activity completely distasteful, instead persuades him to take her to the Semi-Demi Finals of the Woman's Heavyweight Wrestling Championship.

That the fabric of the *Brave New World* is strengthened by needless labor is later born out by Mustapha Mond. "The experiment was tried, more than a century and a half ago," he says, describing why Epsilons work seven-hour days, "The whole of Ireland was put on to the four-hour day. What was the result? Unrest and a large increase in the consumption of soma; that's all" (172).

In *Brave New World*, as in *Invisible Man*, isolation from labor leads inevitably to unrest and instability. The solution? To keep the citizens running by having them perform worthless labor under the auspices that they are contributing to society.

Worthless labor is not the only way that the powers that be in *Invisible Man* and *Brave New World* exercise control over their societies. In both novels, hallucinogenic drugs are perceived as evils that dull the senses and destroy one's sense of urgency and desire for action. In *Brave New World* this comes in the form of soma, a perfect designer drug the citizens consume whenever they have the slightest psychological or physical ill. In many ways, soma represents the perfect form of mind control, as it ultimately dulls all stimuli that would move an individual to independent thought and revolution. In *Invisible Man*, the importance of drugs in suppressing one's individuality and desire for action is not as pronounced as in *Brave New World*, but we see it here and there, particularly in the book's prologue when the narrator talks about a vision he had while smoking marijuana. "I haven't smoked reefer since," he says, "not because they're illegal, but because to see around corners is enough (that is not unusual when you're invisible). But to hear around them is too much; it inhibits action." . . .

In reality, however, it's not really drugs the writers are rallying against, but rather what they symbolize—the ability for any artificial stimuli to distract an individual's attention from a fight for self-assertion. . . .

Both *Invisible Man* and *Brave New World* share common themes as works of literature. Symbolically, they are representative of an individual's fight for recognition and self-determination in a tyrannical society that devalues individual worth. Despite their many similarities, however, the novels seem to diverge in their final opinion of whether the individual has a place in our society. Perhaps this is in the nature of the novels themselves, for each was written with a slightly different intent: *Invisible Man* to inspire greater freedom for all people in an existing American system, and *Brave New World* to inspire fear and loathing towards a possible future system that we still have time to avoid. It is because of this close affinity to our own distinctly American reality that *Invisible Man* offers a ray of hope where *Brave New World* does not. The invisible man must persist, because if he does not, there is no hope for our future. "The thing that Americans have to learn over and over again," said Ellison shortly before his death, "is that they are individuals with individual vision" (Townley 391). It is upon the strengths of these individuals that our entire society is built. And unlike John, the embattled "savage" of *Brave New World*, whose desperation I recognized even as a child peering into a coloring book, the individuals in *Invisible Man* still have the power to make themselves heard and continue the grand cycle of applying their "individual vision" to the tapestry of society.

DAVID GARRETT IZZO ON THE NOVEL'S INFLUENCE AND MEANING

Brave New World (1932) is perhaps the most influential novel of the twentieth century if one sees its impact as not exclusively literary. Huxley's intentions were social, political, economic, psychological, scientific, philosophical, and *then* literary. Many of the ideas in this "novel of ideas" came from his voluminous essays written in the ten years prior to its publication. The influence is wide and deep. . . .

Huxley's novels of ideas are always about moral dilemmas that need to be sorted out. In the 1920s his characters wallow in the philosophy of meaninglessness with sarcasm as their defense veiling a prevalent despair. The characters secretly—or openly—seek a vehicle that can give meaning to a world that has realized that science, technology, and industry are not the answers. Huxley's protagonists evolve as either upward seekers of the perennial philosophy of mysticism, or they devolve into an even greater disaffected nihilism. *Brave New World* was a warning of a future 600 years hence that is already here.

The title comes from Shakespeare:

> O, wonder!
> How many goodly creatures are there here!
> How beauteous mankind is! O brave new world,
> That has such people in't!
>
> *The Tempest*

How influential is Huxley's *Brave New World?* The title, while from *The Tempest*, is recognized today as being from Huxley's novel—these three words are a catchphrase for any person or idea that is cutting edge and may have a possible positive/negative duality. If one Googles "brave new world" (as of 11 May 2006) there are 953,000 hits and the majority are not about Huxley's novel. Examples: "The Brave New World of Customer Centricity," "Mental Health Review, Brave New World," "Iraq embraces a brave new world of democracy," "Brave New World Astrology Alive!," "The Brave New World of E-Showbiz," "Computer Intelligence: A Brave New World," "Politics in a Brave New World," "Koreans Discover Brave New World of Blog," "Brave New World Surf Shop." No other twentieth-century novel title on this planet has become such a ubiquitous term. The meaning of the phrase as Huxley intended is now both ubiquitous and threatening.

Huxley's world is already upon us. Huxley himself recognized it long before the year 2000, first in his introduction to the 1946 edition of *Brave New World*, and then in book-length form for 1958's nonfiction reevaluation *Brave New World Revisited*. This novel, the precursor for the modern genre of science fiction, is still telling the future; the threats it depicts are now more reality than fantasy. "[B]rave new man will be cursed to acquire precisely what he wished for only to discover—painfully and too late—that what he wished for is not exactly what he wanted. Or, Huxley implies . . . he may be so dehumanized that he will not even recognize that in aspiring to be perfect he is no longer even human" (Kass, 52).

In Huxley's *Brave New World* the duality of reason and passion is explicitly out of balance. There is no emotional passion whatsoever. The world is run by Mustapha Mond. "John the Savage" enters this world and almost turns it upside down. To follow, the two square off. Mond: "The world's stable now. People are happy; they get what they want, and they never want what they can't get. They're well off, they're safe; they're never ill; they're not afraid of death; they're blissfully ignorant of passion and old age; they're plagued with no mothers or fathers; they've got no wives or children or lovers to feel strongly about; they're so conditioned that they practically can't help behaving as they ought to behave. And if anything should go wrong, there's soma" (220). Soma is the all-purpose, feel-good drug that fixes everything; a populace in a stupor is not inclined to be rebellious.

John the Savage: "But I don't want comfort. I want God, I want poetry, I want real danger, I want freedom, I want goodness. I want sin." "In fact," said Mustapha Mond, "you're claiming the right to be unhappy." "All right then," said the Savage defiantly, "I'm claiming the right to be unhappy" (240). John is actually claiming the right to have free will, choices, initiative, and spiritual freedom. In this world the people are conditioned to fill and accept certain roles genetically and with "educational" conditioning that amounts to brainwashing. The masses are pacified to believe they want for nothing. All is good—so they think; nothing is bad. There is no sense of comparison. They are lazy, not just of body but also of mind—their ability to think independently has nearly disappeared. While the collective body of the people is pacified, the collective mind is dying into apathy and ignorance. The world is becoming soulless, and without soul and spirit, in Huxley's vision, there will be no progress toward the evolution of consciousness—and that is much more important than being pacified by the constant, sensuous satiety of food, sex, and drugs.

If there is no dark, one cannot truly appreciate the light and think about why the light and dark need to be compared. Light and dark, strong and weak, good and evil have no meaning without contrast and it is from thinking about their meanings that the collective mind moves toward an evolving spiritual consciousness. The mystics call this the reconciliation of opposites. The friction and fission of these opposites rubbing against each other creates the energy needed for consciousness to evolve. Without a reconciliation of opposites the body may be satisfied, but the spirit knows nothing of what it means to be good, strong, heroic and noble. And without this knowledge, life has no meaning. Moreover, the reconciliation of opposites explains the force which Huxley would later call "upward transcendence," the desire to move toward the world of spirit. Downward transcendence is when one thinks too much of one's self and not for the good of the whole. If all good is given instead of chosen, there would be no effort to learn the difference and no progress toward the evolution of consciousness. . . .

Huxley's dear friend D. H. Lawrence, as the character Mark Rampion, was the life force that inhabited Huxley's 1928 novel *Point Counter Point*, and Lawrence is the spirit force that suffuses *Brave New World*. Lawrence died in 1930 in the presence of his wife, Frieda, and Aldous and Maria Huxley, whom he had asked to be with him. Lidan Lin writes, in reviewing Dana Sawyer's *Aldous Huxley: A Biography*:

> Lawrence's influence contributed to the composition of the novel. . . . Huxley shared Lawrence's aversion for the process of industrialization that turns humans into mechanical objects. As Sawyer writes, "[H]ere we find Huxley in agreement with Lawrence who believed that 'men that sit in front of machines, among spinning wheels, in an apotheosis of wheels, often become machines *themselves*.' Both Huxley and Lawrence believed that work . . . can cause us to shirk our first duty to life, which is to live." Sawyer also illuminates the extent to which Huxley's disapproval of H. G. Wells's utopian novel

Men Like Gods, and Henry Ford's autobiography *My Life and Work* spurred the composition of the novel.

In 1929 Huxley met Gerald Heard, who would replace Lawrence as Huxley's best friend. Heard was already deeply involved with his philosophy of humanity being actually a spiritual species that had gone astray from its spiritual underpinnings. Heard affirmed Huxley's deepening interest in mysticism and together they explored the potential for rejuvenating the latent spirit in human beings. Lawrence's lasting influence and Heard's living influence sustained the rest of Huxley's life.

In *Brave New World*, spirit is absent. There is no need for God.

In real life it is tragedy that is in conflict with routine, which gives everyday life its perspective about what is truly important. In a *Brave New World* of ceaseless pacification and sensual pleasure, there is no basis for comparison; stability is maintained, but the spirit's evolution toward consciousness is stalled. Only when individuals, then small groups, then larger groups, then towns, and so on, seek to renew the life of the spirit can humanity reach its destiny.

COLEMAN CARROLL MYRON ON ESCAPE ROUTES IN THE NOVEL

In *Brave New World*, Aldous Huxley responds to specific dictatorships around the globe born out of economic necessity, global warfare, and social chaos by wrestling not only with the root of the issue but also with the complexities that individuals living in such societies face. Although totalitarian manipulation of the masses can take many forms, the result is inertia that stifles both the individual and society. Whereas Huxley is not treating a new idea, for societies have placed people in chains of conformity to safeguard the nation state since the beginning of time, he is asking at what cost should systems endure in which the motives of a select, enlightened, self-interested minority rule over the majority? In the characters of John the Savage, Bernard Marx, and Helmholtz Watson, Huxley considers choices of escape that the undernourished majority may be forced to take when controlled by the smaller yet better fed members of society. Whereas Huxley knows that the vast majority strictly controlled by society will not budge from their couches of complacency, some few will recognize their conditions and seek out that which will sustain them regardless of the cost[.] . . .

Although the devil per se is not present in a world void of God, for the Brave New World dwellers the devil represents those moments when an Alpha or Beta frees his or her mind from the party line that "everyone belongs to everyone" and recognizes individuality. Unfortunately, for the greater part of the society, these moments that allow for reflection and for pause do not happen often enough, because the Protestant work ethic which drives this society has everyone focused on moving forward to the next feelie (pornographic film) or conquest, rather than stopping to connect with other people or to question what's important in life. Those conformists to the state form a personhood that positions them as being responsible for conducting themselves in the business of the state, which itself is a work in progress; whereas, those who do stop to formulate some sense of their surroundings are identified quickly and shipped off to Icelandic exile, no longer able to be a danger to the rest of society. . . .

After providing an overview in the first two chapters of the current world state that emphasizes how the "World Controllers" program happiness through prenatal treatment, drugs, and hypnotic suggestions, Huxley shifts his emphasis to Bernard Marx, Helmholtz Watson, and John the Savage, three individuals who aren't doped up on soma and oblivious to the controls placed on them by society. In freeing themselves from the mind-numbing motto of the Brave New World society, "Conformity, Identity, and Stability," these nonconformists forge their own identity and selfhood apart from the state, where everyone who conforms is part of the mechanism of capitalistic society and of the Protestant work ethic run amok.

Because they seek change, these individuals will face exile from this community since their mere presence and thoughts create instability.

In the character of Bernard Marx, Huxley catapults the reader further into the theme behind his novel; for in the naming of Bernard Marx, Huxley draws upon the name of Karl Marx, author (along with Friedrich Engels) of *Das Kapital* who denounces capitalist society. Whereas Karl Marx challenged capitalism from a philosophical viewpoint, Bernard Marx lashes out at the Brave New World society because it proves hostile to him. From a conversation between Lenina and Fanny, the reader learns that Bernard has a bad "reputation" because "he doesn't like Obstacle Golf" and because "he spends most of his time by himself—*alone*" (*BNW* 44). Aside from the information that other characters reveal, Marx himself admits to being disgusted with society's view of Lenina as a piece of "meat" (45), of her belonging to everyone else. In addition to these dislikes, which could possibly be attributed to the fact that "somebody made a mistake when he was still in the bottle—thought he was a Gamma and put alcohol into his blood surrogate" (46), Marx represents a failed component of the Brave New World society, in that he, an Alpha male, when in contact "with members of the lower castes always [is] reminded . . . painfully of . . . physical inadequacy. 'I am I, and wish I wasn't'; his self-consciousness was acute and distressing. Each time he found himself looking on the level, instead of downward, into a Delta's face, he felt humiliated . . . the laughter of the women to whom he made proposals, [and] the practical joking of his equals among the men . . . made him feel an outsider; and feeling an outsider he behaved like one, which increased the prejudice against him and intensified the contempt and hostility aroused by his physical defects" (64–65). The fact that Marx does not relish his membership in the society leads to his discontent with it, and, in turn, to his aloneness and appreciation for the beauty of nature. Although he makes disparaging comments and is bitter about the state of affairs, he does nothing when faced with adversity and tries to piggyback onto the efforts of others who do fight: "And suddenly there was Helmholtz at [John's] side—'Good old Helmholtz!'—also punching . . . [and] throwing the poison out by handfuls through the open window. . . . 'They're done for,' said Bernard and, urged by a sudden impulse, ran forward to help them; then thought better of it and halted; then, ashamed, stepped forward again; then again thought better of it, and was standing in an agony of humiliated indecision" (219–220). His reluctance to act on his ideas brandishes him as a coward and a hypocrite. Despite his reluctance to act, he is still recognized as a partner in crime with the other two heroes, which resigns him to a fate, foreshadowed earlier in the novel, of exile to Iceland.

Unlike Bernard Marx, Helmholtz Watson, his friend and fellow soul searcher, is not an outcast in society and recognizes that his mental capacity and individuality sets him apart from other human beings. He is the "Escalator-Squash champion, [an] indefatigable lover (. . . six hundred and forty different girls in under four years) . . . [an] admirable committee man and best mixer" (67). Yet like Bernard, he recognizes all too recently his indifference to those in civilization and "sport, women, [and] communal activities were only, so far as he was concerned, second bests" (67). As he tells Bernard, "I've been cutting all my committees and all my girls. You can't imagine what a hullabaloo they've been making about it at the College. Still, it's been worth it, I think" (68–69). Aside from steering clear of his willing role as consumer of sex and sport, Helmholtz, as a lecturer at the college of emotional engineering, has been diverging from orders to write phrases that adhere to the company line in order to write ones containing "a bit of propaganda . . . [that] engineer[s] [the students] into feeling as I'd felt / when I wrote the rhymes" (183–184). Specifically, Helmholtz wants to write phrases that require students to look inside themselves to discover what is within: "Did you ever feel . . . as though you had something inside you that was only waiting for you to give it a chance to come out? Some sort of extra power that you aren't using— you know, like all the water that goes down the falls instead of through the turbines?" In admitting to having "a queer feeling . . . that I've got something important to say and the power to say it—only I don't know what it is, and I can't make any use of the power" (69), Helmholtz shows that he has advanced more than Marx because he is able to articulate his selfhood when he joins with John the Savage in the soma incident and when he creates a poem that celebrates silence and the presence of a spiritual being. As a direct result of the incident with John, Helmholtz is exiled to the Falkland Islands, where, as the Controller explained to him earlier, "he'll meet the most interesting set of men and women to be found anywhere in the world. All the people who, for one reason or another, have got too self-consciously individual to fit into community-life. All the people who aren't satisfied with orthodoxy, who've got independent ideas of their own. Everyone, in a word, who's any one. I almost envy you, Mr. Watson" (233). For Helmholtz, his exile gives him the freedom to pursue his interests without the interference of the nation state.

Finally, in the character of John the Savage, Huxley gives the reader the outsider in civilization, the one who is to provide understanding to the situation. Not only is John the outsider to the Brave New World, but also to those on the "Savage Reservation." On the reservation, John's *persona non gratis* status is because his mother is a former inhabitant of the new world who—from the old world's perspective—prostitutes herself. His mother's amoral behavior and her present circumstances as a woman of the new world shift to her son John who is despised and chastised by his peers on the reservation. This inheritance that Linda gives to John also makes John an outsider in the new world, where natural birth by a mother is abhorrent. As an oddity in the new world, John befriends Bernard Marx who identifies in the other the great pangs of loneliness that each feels because of the way that people perceive them: "Bernard blushed uncomfortably. 'You see,' he said, mumbling and with averted eyes, 'I'm rather different from most people, I suppose. If one happens to be decanted different. . . . Yes, that's just it.' The young man nodded. 'If one's different, one's bound to be lonely. They're beastly to one. Do you know, they shut me out of absolutely everything? When the other boys were sent out to spend the night on the mountains—you know, when you have to dream which your sacred animal is—they wouldn't tell me any of the secrets . . . '" (139).

After failing to effect change by tossing out the soma, John attempts a more philosophical approach through a conversation with Mustapha Mond, the freethinking world controller. Together they discuss the price of happiness. John focuses on the price of happiness: freedom and individual expression, while basing his argument on Shakespearean thought. World Controller Mond states that society has had to suppress feelings, beauty, and truth in order to maintain a stable, thriving society. And he says of this particular work [Shakespeare], which "people used to call high art," that the ideas it cultivates do not fuel society and are sacrificed in favor of products that "don't mean anything" but do provide immediate satisfaction: feelies, scent organs, obstacle golf, drugs, and ritual (226–227). When the conversation shifts to the absence of religion from present society, Mond points out that God has been tossed from the picture because civilization is so stable that no one has the need to reach out for a God since every need that it has is immediately provided. Through systematic control of society and the elimination of aspects of it that do not maintain stability, the Brave New World creates an immobile society where everyone is conditioned to be happy. In spite of this utopian society, John makes his decision:

> "But I don't want comfort, I want God, I want poetry, I want real danger, I want freedom, I want goodness, I want sin."
>
> "In fact, said Mustapha Mond, "you're claiming the right to be unhappy."
>
> "Not to mention the right to grow old, and ugly and impotent . . ." [246].

John's decision, foreshadowed earlier by his tossing out of the soma, revolves around the idea that he would rather be unhappy than live his life superficially.

His retreat to the lighthouse marks a desire to repent for his ways; yet, even in this environment, John is hounded by the all-pervasive arm of a society concerned only with its efficiency. As John attempts to find selfhood and purge himself from the effects of civilization, Darwin Bonaparte captures his self-flagellation on film in *The Savage of Surrey*, a product of the capitalist scheme to make a product at anyone's expense. John's eventual suicide signifies to the Brave New World society that this world, which has restricted his individual freedom and dignity, is one in which he cannot live and maintain his self-hood. Although he would have relished the opportunity to be banished as his friends Bernard and Helmholtz were, it wasn't an option for him since society controls and maintains his work or position.

With the death of John and the banishment of Helmholtz and Marx, the Brave New World returns to normalcy and can continue forward while maintaining its immobility. At all levels, *Brave New World* operates to satisfy the community that wraps itself around the cog of capitalism and the Protestant work ethic that denies the self and selfhood in all manners and forms.

SCOTT PELLER ON "FORDISM" IN *BRAVE NEW WORLD*

Huxley's novel exposes the foundation of Fordist economics as necessitating the maintenance and reproduction of workers engaged in repetitive job tasks.[3] The goals of happiness and contentment for workers through their enjoyment of their labor serve to ensure security, peace, and stability for the ruling Alpha elites. While Huxley's satire takes Fordism to task for reducing the intellectual aspirations of the Alphas to the banality of dancing to the music of the Sexophonists and participating in the Orgy-porgy, his novel also reveals the exploitation of the toiling masses in achieving this secure world for the elites. In World Controller Mond's model of the perfect society, the eight-ninths of the population living below the water are required in order for the one-ninth to remain on top of the iceberg (*Brave New World* 268). For Mond, the eight-ninths are the stupid masses that are content and happy while the top one-ninth are supposed to be the ones whose superior breeding must be kept in check by the controllers.[4]

By the end of the 1920s, American industry and consumer culture had come to dominate the Western world: "THE FUTURE OF AMERICA is the future of the world. Material circumstances are driving all nations along the path in which America is going" (Huxley, "Outlook for American Culture" 186). Huxley's critique of the "material circumstances" embodied in 1920s America appears in *Brave New World* through the depictions of a society predicated on abundance, mandatory guilt-free sexual relations, a caste system based on knowledge limits, and the ongoing insipid music, dancing, and sense-appealing entertainments. Huxley locates this drive toward conformity and the banality of mass culture in the mass-production manufacturing and assembly process fathered by Henry Ford and expressed in the development of the Model T automobile. For Huxley, the America driving the material circumstances is an economic, social, and cultural phenomenon identified as Fordism.[5]

Fordism is a capitalist method for securing uninterrupted production. Through the initiatives of the $5/day, eight-hour workday, means such as the Sociological Department, English school and Americanization program meant to control the lives of workers inside and outside the factory, Fordism addressed the requirements of the market for the reproduction of laborers and the fulfillment of steady production. *Brave New World* is a critique of this streamlining process, of its all-too-pragmatic father Henry Ford, and finally of the Fordist workers whose lives of repetitive labor and goals of material comfort appeared to have triumphed over notions of intellectual inquiry and self-reflection.

Fordism is named for automobile manufacturer Henry Ford. Ford appears in *Brave New World* in the dominating form of Our Ford, the father and Holy Ghost of the decanted world. . . .

The common theme in Ford's pronouncements that most irked Huxley was the idea that the arts and intellectual endeavor were unnecessary and wasteful. Ford's infamous remark that history was more or less bunk prompted Huxley to write: "The saint of the new dispensation has no choice but to hate history. And not history only. If he is logical he must hate literature, philosophy, pure science, the arts—all the mental activities that distract mankind from an acquisitive interest in objects. 'Bunk' was the term of abuse selected by Mr. Ford for disparaging history. Bunk: for how can even serious and philosophical history be enlightening? History is the account of people who lived before such things as machine tools and joint-stock banks had been invented" (*Music at Night* 131–2).

Imagination and intellectual endeavor not employed for the betterment of the human race through improved efficiency and business practices was considered wasteful. Irrational thoughts, artistic endeavors, the search for philosophical truth and poetic beauty, prove worthless in the business world promoted and dominated by Ford.

During the nineteenth century, tool making in the United States was evolving into an ever-more-systematic process. . . .

By the turn of the century, the systemization of production had become the province of a former mid-level engineer named Frederick Winslow Taylor. In Taylorized production the worker's knowledge or craft experience become more an obstacle than a requirement for performing the job task. The job task is reduced to the point of one or two steps performed repeatedly by the worker throughout the day. Taylor's ideal worker needed to be strong as an ox and as stupid as one.[10]

At the Highland Park factory, Henry Ford implemented many of Taylor's production initiatives such as the time study used to determine how much time and how many workers were required to perform a certain task.[11] Ford's factories became the definitive example of rationalized labor in terms of the reduction of unnecessary physical movement by workers as well as unnecessary mental activity: "The essence of scientific management was systematic separation of the mental component of commodity production from the manual. The functions of thinking and deciding were what management sought to wrest from the worker, so that the manual efforts of wage earners might be directed in detail by a 'superior intelligence'" (Montgomery 252).

Ford's installation of the moving assembly line represented the monotonous and fast-paced job tasks of the twentieth-century factory. The incentive of high wages, nearly double the going wage by 1914 standards, was meant to solve Ford's employee turnover problem and to produce social stability through which employees would see themselves less as workers and more as consumers.[12] Thus, through Ford's efforts, a universal car, the Model T, was mass-produced by a consistent workforce at an ever-faster rate and for sale at an ever-lower price. . . .

As with Ford's attempts at manufacturing a dependable, reproducible workforce, Huxley's novel provides its own version of Fordism. We see the manufacturing of embryos on an assembly line, the constant drive at improving efficiency, the regulation of future workers through a version of the English school and Sociological Department, and a maintaining of worker stability through the leisure-time pursuits of consumer culture.

In the first three chapters of *Brave New World*, Huxley presents the manufacturing process of embryos through a guided tour of a reproduction factory. It is on this tour that the Bokanovsky Process for the mass reproduction of workers is explained:

> Standard men and women; in uniform batches. The whole of a small factory staffed with the products of a single bokanovskified egg. 'Ninety-six identical twins working ninety-six identical machines!' [6–7].

Within the hatchery the physical reproduction of workers has become the commodity for rationalized production on the assembly line. The laborers are no longer even required to participate in the physical reproduction of themselves as the old-fashioned method of conception through physical exchange has been replaced with a reproducible formula of biological determinism. This biological determinism has been developed to the point that embryonic laborers are reproduced based on the job tasks required. Through their predetermined biological mixtures these embryos are conditioned to belong to one of five castes: Alpha, Beta, Gamma, Delta, or Epsilon. The Alpha embryos have been produced and will in turn be educated to assume the highest leadership positions within the World State. The Beta, Gamma, Delta, and Epsilon embryos will be segregated and educated to be contented in accordance with their respective lots in life.

Each of these castes is produced and conditioned to be slightly less physically and intellectually enamored by degrees than their superior class or classes. The Epsilons, at the bottom of the system, are stunted and stupefied by oxygen depriva- tion and chemical treatments. They have been produced to perform the lowest menial job tasks and to be contented with their position. The Epsilons are the epitome of the ideal Tayl- orized worker (15). The future lower-caste workers are manu- factured with attributes for specific job tasks, climates, and hazardous environments. Some are produced to withstand the heat of mines and steel plants while future chemical workers are "trained in the toleration of lead, caustic soda, tar, chlorine" (18). Other future Epsilons are manufactured in a hoist in order to be able to live and work comfortably on space jets while they are in flight: "They learn to associate topsy-turvydom with well-being; in fact, they're only truly happy when they're standing on their heads" (18–9).

As individual units the Epsilons are as easily replaceable as a lug nut, but as a collectivity engaged in job tasks they are indispensable. By virtue of their decanting they are not seem- ingly capable of realizing the dangers of their physical labor nor are they able to desire a more fulfilling existence. The triumph of the biological determinism in *Brave New World* is the acceptance, by all castes, of the intentional production of dumb and expendable workers. "Huxley's Deltas and Epsilons are the equivalents of Taylor's gorillas and human oxen. They are deliberately bred to be just intelligent enough to do the job they are predestined for, and to be too stupid to understand or want to understand anything else" (Firchow 108).

The tour of the hatchery also reveals the drive of Fordism to continually look for ways of eliminating waste and improve the efficiency of the reproduction factory. The following exchange between the director of hatcheries and conditioning and Henry Foster reveals this agenda:

"The lower the caste," said Mr. Foster, "the shorter the oxygen." The first organ affected was the brain. After that the skeleton. At seventy per cent of normal oxygen you got dwarfs. At less than seventy eyeless monsters. "Who are no use at all . . ." [15].

The comment by Foster that the eyeless monsters "are no use at all" demonstrates the endgame for human reproduction—use value. One suspects that if eyeless monsters could be used in some menial application that they too would be mass-produced. As with the time-study engineers at the Ford Highland Park factory, the director and Foster strive for and marvel at the efficiency of streamlined production. One senses in the above discussion the constant drive for improving the process through the reduction in time as Foster beams at the prospect of shortening the maturation process.

As with the process for the physical reproduction of workers, ideological methods of education and indoctrination are applied to growing children to confirm and maintain their respective social identities. During the tour of the hatchery, examples of the educational conditioning are manifested. In the nursery the students observe a group of Delta infants being educated to dislike books and flowers. This aversion therapy, the director maintains, helps to reduce thinking by the Deltas and enforces the values of the Delta children to become pleasant consumers. The students then observe the methods used to instruct children in the proper morals of the New World as they sleep. They enter a room in which older children are asleep; a whispering voice is heard repeating a lesson in "Elementary Class Consciousness." "Oh no, I don't want to play with Delta children. And Epsilons are still worse" (30–1).

With a similar purpose as the Ford Sociological Department, Americanization program, and English school, the Elementary Class Consciousness program is meant to educate workers in their future roles as workers and consumers. This conditioning does not stop once the children are adults. The lower, non-Alpha castes are modeled on Ford's productive terms in that they labor for seven hours a day and then are provided pleasures during their leisure time. While World Controller Mond contends that they like it ("it's light, it's childishly simple"), the necessity for "soma" and the "feelies" reveals that the lower castes are not completely content but still require ideological control. The entertainments and media are constructed to dispense the proper ideological content for the targeted group. As such, each group reads the newspapers made available for them and listens to *their* radio programs. The practice of these lifelong methods of conditioning suggests that indeed even biologically produced workers require ideological maintenance.

Brave New World is a world dominated by Fordism in which workers achieved permanent happiness through biological conditioning, job performance and leisure time to purchase commodities and pleasures. The dystopian focus is on providing uninterrupted production, which is for the most part mediated not through the violence of a repressive apparatus but rather through ideological conditioning and steady ideological reinforcement. The mass consciousness being constantly reinforced in Huxley's novel is Huxley's fear of Fordism run amok. It is the attainment of the perfect product (the human being) and the requirements of the job tasks that have themselves become perfected and unchanging.

Notes

3. "Huxley never showed much understanding of or sympathy for the working class" (Baker 85). [Editor's note: There is much evidence to dispute Baker's assertion in Huxley's fiction, nonfiction, and biography both before and after *Brave New World*. One example: in his 1928 novel, *Point Counter Point*, Huxley valorizes the working class through his D. H. Lawrence character, Mark Rampion.]

4. "The problem is only with the alphas, that one-ninth of the population, left with the capacity to think for themselves" (Ramamurty 70).

5. I am limiting my analysis of Fordism to the period preceding and influencing Huxley's work, namely the Model-T era of the 1920s. For information on the locating of Fordism as a post–World War II development, refer to Nick Heffernan, *Capital, Class and Technology in Contemporary American Culture: Projecting Post-Fordism* (London: Pluto, 2000) and Nelson Lichtenstein, *Walter Reuther: The Most Dangerous Man in Detroit* (Urbana and Chicago, IL: University of Illinois Press, 1995).

10. Hounshell 15.

11. That combination of stupidity and brute force is embodied in the worker on whom Taylor modeled his representation of the worker, a little Pennsylvania Dutch man called Schmidt. However, as Martha Banta points out, "No such person as Schmidt existed to be taught 'the science of shoveling' pig iron. Taylor made up his story based on a very different kind of worker, one Henry Noll, but the imaginary Schmidt furthered Taylor's thesis: getting the right man 'to handle 47 tons of pig iron per day and making him glad to do it.' A mix of pleasantries and tough talk accomplishes what *the boss* wants (more goods produced at lower costs) and what *the worker* wants (higher wages)" (Banta 114–5).

12. "The epitome of mass production was the Detroit-area Highland Park plant. There, unlike the older vertical production structures marked by skilled workers assembling cars in teams by hand, a modern horizontal plant layout allowed workers to remain stationary while the parts and components moved around them" (Pietrykowski 385).

Works by Aldous Huxley

Novels

Crome Yellow, 1921.

Mortal Coils, 1922.

Antic Hay, 1923.

Young Archimedes, 1924.

Those Barren Leaves, 1925.

Point Counter Point, 1928.

Leda, 1929.

The World of Light, 1931.

Brave New World, 1932.

Eyeless in Gaza,1936.

After Many a Summer Dies the Swan, 1939.

Time Must Have a Stop, 1944.

Ape and Essence, 1948.

The Devils of Loudun, 1952.

The Doors of Perception, 1954.

Genius and Goddess, 1955.

Heaven and Hell, 1956.

After the Fireworks, 1957.

Brave New World Revisited, 1958.

Island, 1962.

The Crows of Pearblossom, 1967.

Jacob's Hands, with Christopher Isherwood, 1998.

Poetry and Short Story Collections

The Burning Wheel: Poems, 1916.

The Defeat of Youth: And Other Poems, 1918.

Limbo, 1918.

Selected Poems, 1925.

Two or Three Graces: And Other Stories, 1926.

Arabia Infelix and Other Poems, 1929.

Do What You Will, 1929.

Brief Candles, 1930.

The Cicadas: And Other Poems, 1931.

Rotunda: A Selection of His Work, 1932.

Texts and Pretexts, 1933.

The Olive Tree: And Other Essays, 1936.

Ends and Means, 1937.

Brave New World and Brave New World Revisited, 1942.

Stories, Essays and Poems, 1942.

Little Mexican: Six Stories, 1948.

Themes and Variations, 1950.

Tomorrow and Tomorrow and Tomorrow: And Other Essays, 1956.

The Art of Seeing, 1957.

The Collected Poetry of Aldous Huxley, 1971.

The World of Aldous Huxley: An Omnibus of His Fiction and Non-Fiction Over Three Decades, 1971.

The Doors of Perception and Heaven and Hell: Vol. 1, 1972.

Nonfiction

On the Margin, 1923.

Along the Road: Notes and Essays of a Tourist, 1925.

Essays New and Old, 1926.

Proper Studies, 1928.

Holy Face and Other Essays, 1929.

Vulgarity in Literature: Digressions from a Theme, 1930.

The Letters of D. H. Lawrence, 1932.

Jesting Pilate: The Diary of a Journey, 1932.

Beyond the Mexique Bay, 1934.

The Elder Peter Bruegel 1528(?)–1569, with Jean Videpoche 1938.

Grey Eminence: A Study in Religion and Politics, 1941.

The Perennial Philosophy, 1945.

Science, Liberty and Peace, 1946.

ADONIS and the Alphabet: and Other Essays, 1956.

On Art and Artists, 1960.

Aldous Huxley: A Collection of Critical Essays, 1968.

Letters of Aldous Huxley, 1969.

Moksha: Aldous Huxley's Classic Writings on Psychedelics and the Visionary Experience 1931–1963, 1980.

Complete Essays, Volume 3 1930–1935, 2000.

Annotated Bibliography

Baker, Robert S. *Brave New World: History, Science, and Dystopia*. Boston: Twayne, 1990.

In this volume, Robert S. Baker discusses the political implications of *Brave New World* and its relevance to the twentieth century.

———. *The Dark Historic Page: Social Satire and Historicism in the Novels of Aldous Huxley 1921–1939*. Madison: University of Wisconsin Press, 1982.

In this study, Baker investigates the role of Darwinism and scientific progression as the historical backdrop for Huxley's futuristic novel.

Bradshaw, David. *The Hidden Huxley*. London: Faber & Faber, 1994.

This volume contains a collection of Huxley's insights and opinions on the issues of his time and tries to argue for a distinct evolution in Huxley's thinking.

Deery, June. *Aldous Huxley and the Mysticism of Science*. New York: St. Martin's Press, 1996.

Deery analyzes Huxley's use and knowledge of science as he applied it to literary fiction. This volume also traces Huxley's influence on popular culture and how he has contributed to interdisciplinary debates on religion, literature, and science.

Firchow, Peter. *The End of Utopia: A Study of Aldous Huxley's Brave New World*. Lewisburg, Pa.: Bucknell UP, 1984.

Firchow discusses his interpretation of *Brave New World*'s assessment of the future and reflects on the questions Huxley raises in the novel.

Gleason, Abbott, Jack Goldsmith, and Martha C. Nussbaum, eds. *Nineteen Eighty-Four: Orwell and Our Future*. Princeton, N.J.: Princeton UP, 2005.

George Orwell and Aldous Huxley are frequently discussed in the same context and seen as addressing similar concerns. Although this volume is mainly focused on Orwell, two distinguished critics contribute commentary on Huxley where his ideas overlap and contrast with those of Orwell.

Izzo, David Garrett, and Kim Kirkpatrick, eds. *Huxley's "Brave New World": Essays.* Jefferson, N.C., and London: McFarland & Company, 2008.

In his introduction, editor David Garrett Izzo suggests that *Brave New World* can be judged as the most influential novel of the twentieth century because of its wide-ranging focus on social, political, philosophical, economic, psychological, and literary ideas. Huxley's imagined utopia was set 600 years in the future, but Izzo, along with many other critics, find alarming similarities in our twenty-first-century life with the author's disturbing prophecies. The volume contains 14 essays on these observations.

Larsen, Peter M. "Synthetic Myths in Aldous Huxley's *Brave New World*: A Note." *English Studies* 62 (1981): 506–508.

In this essay, Larsen defines the synthetic myth and discusses its importance to the "fictional universe" of *Brave New World*.

McGiveron, Rafeeq O. "Huxley's *Brave New World*." *The Explicator* 57, Issue 1 (Fall 1998): 27.

McGiveron examines Huxley's use of ironic allusion with respect to the names of the characters in *Brave New World*. He discusses the double meanings and political and literary implications of the characters' names.

Nance, Guinevera A. *Aldous Huxley.* New York: Continuum, 1988.

Nance devotes a chapter to *Brave New World*, providing summary and critical analysis, with an emphasis on the moral implications of the Savage.

Contributors

Harold Bloom is Sterling Professor of the Humanities at Yale University. Educated at Cornell and Yale universities, he is the author of more than 30 books, including *Shelley's Mythmaking* (1959), *The Visionary Company* (1961), *Blake's Apocalypse* (1963), *Yeats* (1970), *The Anxiety of Influence* (1973), *A Map of Misreading* (1975), *Kabbalah and Criticism* (1975), *Agon: Toward a Theory of Revisionism* (1982), *The American Religion* (1992), *The Western Canon* (1994), *Omens of Millennium: The Gnosis of Angels, Dreams, and Resurrection* (1996), *Shakespeare: The Invention of the Human* (1998), *How to Read and Why* (2000), *Genius: A Mosaic of One Hundred Exemplary Creative Minds* (2002), *Hamlet: Poem Unlimited* (2003), *Where Shall Wisdom Be Found?* (2004), and *Jesus and Yahweh: The Names Divine* (2005). In addition, he is the author of hundreds of articles, reviews, and editorial introductions. In 1999, Professor Bloom received the American Academy of Arts and Letters' Gold Medal for Criticism. He has also received the International Prize of Catalonia, the Alfonso Reyes Prize of Mexico, and the Hans Christian Andersen Bicentennial Prize of Denmark.

Rudolf B. Schmerl is a retired faculty member of the University of Michigan,

Cristie L. March is associated with the University of North Carolina at Chapel Hill. Her research interests have focused on Anglo-Indian, Caribbean, and Scottish literatures and theories of gender.

Robert L. Mack is the author of *Thomas Gray: A Life* (2000).

Cass R. Sunstein is a distinguished scholar and lawyer with expertise on constitutional law, the First Amendment, and jurisprudence. He is Karl N. Llewellyn Professor of Jurisprudence at the University of Chicago Law School and is also associated with the department of political science.

Richard A. Posner is the author of *Law and Literature* (1998) and *Public Intellectuals: A Study of Decline* (2001). He is also a judge, U. S. court of appeals for the seventh circuit, and is a senior lecturer at the University of Chicago Law School.

Carey Snyder teaches in the English department at Ohio University. She is the author of *British Fiction and Cross-Cultural Encounters: Ethnographic Modernism from Wells to Woolf* (2002).

John Coughlin has taught at Oakland University in Rochester, Michigan.

David Garrett Izzo has extensively published work on twentieth-century British and American literature. He is the director of the English program and a professor of English at American Public University.

Coleman Carroll Myron teaches in the English department at American Public University.

Scott Peller teaches African-American literature at Wayne State University.

Acknowledgments

Rudolf B. Schmerl, "The Two Future Worlds of Aldous Huxley." From *PMLA* 77, no. 3 (June 1962): 328–29. Copyright © 1962 *PMLA*.

Cristie L. March, "A Dystopic Vision of Gender in Aldous Huxley's *Brave New World* (1932)." From *Women in Literature: Reading Through the Lens of Gender*, edited by Jerilyn Fisher and Ellen S. Silber, pp. 53–55. Published by Greenwood Press. Copyright © 2003 by Jerilyn Fisher and Ellen S. Silber.

Robert L. Mack, "Another Thomas Gray Parody in Aldous Huxley's *Brave New World*." From *Notes and Queries* 51, no. 2 (June 2004): 178–82. Copyright © 2004 *Notes and Queries*.

Cass R. Sunstein, "Sexual and Political Freedom." From *On Nineteen Eighty-Four: Orwell and Our Future*, edited by Abbott Gleason, Jack Goldsmith, and Martha C. Nussbaum, pp. 235, 238–41. Copyright © 2005 by Princeton University Press.

Richard A. Posner, "Orwell Versus Huxley: *Brave New World*." From *On Nineteen Eighty-Four: Orwell and Our Future*, edited by Abbott Gleason, Jack Goldsmith, and Martha C. Nussbaum, pp. 191–95. Copyright © 2005 by Princeton University Press.

Carey Snyder, "'When the Indian Was in Vogue': D. H. Lawrence, Aldous Huxley, and Ethnological Tourism in the Southwest." From *Modern Fiction Studies* 53, no. 4 (2007): 664, 677–79, 682–83, 689–90. Copyright © 2007 by the Purdue Research Foundation.

John Coughlin, "*Brave New World* and Ralph Ellison's *Invisible Man*." From *Huxley's Brave New World: Essays*, edited by David Garrett Izzo and Kim Kirkpatrick, pp. 88–91, 94.

Index

viviparous reproduction, 26

W
Ward, Mary Humphrey, 12
The Waste Land (Eliot), 8
women, in *Brave New World*, 73–75
work ethic, 105, 110

working class, 20, 116n3
World Controllers, 28, 105
world's fairs, 92, 93
World State, 19, 23, 30–31, 70–71, 114
World War I, 14, 30–31
World War II, 7, 10, 14